The Philosophy of Bird Watching

By

Neil Holmes

Thanks

Thanks to my wife, Larissa, for introducing me to such a relaxing and fascinating hobby. Movement in the trees, bushes, and further afield can mean only one thing: a fine feathered friend is living life as it should be lived; free! Now, where are my binoculars before it flies away…

Contents

3

The Raven

By <u>Edgar Allan Poe</u>

Once upon a midnight dreary, while I pondered, weak and
weary,
Over many a quaint and curious volume of forgotten lore—
While I nodded, nearly napping, suddenly there came a tapping,
As of someone gently rapping, rapping at my chamber door.
"'Tis some visitor," I muttered, "tapping at my chamber door—
Only this and nothing more."

Ah, distinctly I remember it was in the bleak December;
And each separate dying ember wrought its ghost upon the
floor.
Eagerly I wished the morrow;—vainly I had sought to borrow
From my books surcease of sorrow—sorrow for the lost
Lenore—
For the rare and radiant maiden whom the angels name
Lenore—
Nameless *here* for evermore.

And the silken, sad, uncertain rustling of each purple curtain
Thrilled me—filled me with fantastic terrors never felt before;
So that now, to still the beating of my heart, I stood repeating
"'Tis some visitor entreating entrance at my chamber door—
Some late visitor entreating entrance at my chamber door;—
This it is and nothing more."

Presently my soul grew stronger; hesitating then no longer,
"Sir," said I, "or Madam, truly your forgiveness I implore;
But the fact is I was napping, and so gently you came rapping,
And so faintly you came tapping, tapping at my chamber door,
That I scarce was sure I heard you"—here I opened wide the
door;—
Darkness there and nothing more.

Deep into that darkness peering, long I stood there wondering,
fearing,
Doubting, dreaming dreams no mortal ever dared to dream
before;
But the silence was unbroken, and the stillness gave no token,
And the only word there spoken was the whispered word,
"Lenore?"
This I whispered, and an echo murmured back the word,
"Lenore!"—
Merely this and nothing more.

Back into the chamber turning, all my soul within me burning,
Soon again I heard a tapping somewhat louder than before.
"Surely," said I, "surely that is something at my window lattice;
Let me see, then, what thereat is, and this mystery explore—
Let my heart be still a moment and this mystery explore;—
'Tis the wind and nothing more!"

Open here I flung the shutter, when, with many a flirt and
flutter,
In there stepped a stately Raven of the saintly days of yore;
Not the least obeisance made he; not a minute stopped or stayed
he;
But, with mien of lord or lady, perched above my chamber
door—
Perched upon a bust of Pallas just above my chamber door—
Perched, and sat, and nothing more.

Then this ebony bird beguiling my sad fancy into smiling,
By the grave and stern decorum of the countenance it wore,
"Though thy crest be shorn and shaven, thou," I said, "art sure
no craven,
Ghastly grim and ancient Raven wandering from the Nightly
shore—
Tell me what thy lordly name is on the Night's Plutonian
shore!"
Quoth the Raven "Nevermore."

Much I marvelled this ungainly fowl to hear discourse so
plainly,
Though its answer little meaning—little relevancy bore;
For we cannot help agreeing that no living human being
Ever yet was blessed with seeing bird above his chamber
door—
Bird or beast upon the sculptured bust above his chamber door,
With such name as "Nevermore."

But the Raven, sitting lonely on the placid bust, spoke only
That one word, as if his soul in that one word he did outpour.
Nothing farther then he uttered—not a feather then he
fluttered—
Till I scarcely more than muttered "Other friends have flown
before—
On the morrow *he* will leave me, as my Hopes have flown
before."
Then the bird said "Nevermore."

Startled at the stillness broken by reply so aptly spoken,
"Doubtless," said I, "what it utters is its only stock and store
Caught from some unhappy master whom unmerciful Disaster
Followed fast and followed faster till his songs one burden
bore—
Till the dirges of his Hope that melancholy burden bore
Of 'Never—nevermore'."

But the Raven still beguiling all my fancy into smiling,
Straight I wheeled a cushioned seat in front of bird, and bust
and door;
Then, upon the velvet sinking, I betook myself to linking
Fancy unto fancy, thinking what this ominous bird of yore—
What this grim, ungainly, ghastly, gaunt, and ominous bird of
yore
Meant in croaking "Nevermore."

This I sat engaged in guessing, but no syllable expressing
To the fowl whose fiery eyes now burned into my bosom's
core;

This and more I sat divining, with my head at ease reclining
On the cushion's velvet lining that the lamp-light gloated o'er,
But whose velvet-violet lining with the lamp-light gloating o'er,
    She shall press, ah, nevermore!

Then, methought, the air grew denser, perfumed from an unseen
            censer
Swung by Seraphim whose foot-falls tinkled on the tufted floor.
"Wretch," I cried, "thy God hath lent thee—by these angels he
            hath sent thee
Respite—respite and nepenthe from thy memories of Lenore;
Quaff, oh quaff this kind nepenthe and forget this lost Lenore!"
            Quoth the Raven "Nevermore."

"Prophet!" said I, "thing of evil!—prophet still, if bird or
            devil!—
Whether Tempter sent, or whether tempest tossed thee here
            ashore,
Desolate yet all undaunted, on this desert land enchanted—
On this home by Horror haunted—tell me truly, I implore—
Is there—*is* there balm in Gilead?—tell me—tell me, I
            implore!"
            Quoth the Raven "Nevermore."

"Prophet!" said I, "thing of evil!—prophet still, if bird or devil!
By that Heaven that bends above us—by that God we both
            adore—
Tell this soul with sorrow laden if, within the distant Aidenn,
It shall clasp a sainted maiden whom the angels name Lenore—
Clasp a rare and radiant maiden whom the angels name
            Lenore."
            Quoth the Raven "Nevermore."

"Be that word our sign of parting, bird or fiend!" I shrieked,
            upstarting—
"Get thee back into the tempest and the Night's Plutonian
            shore!
Leave no black plume as a token of that lie thy soul hath
            spoken!

Leave my loneliness unbroken!—quit the bust above my door!
Take thy beak from out my heart, and take thy form from off
my door!"
Quoth the Raven "Nevermore."

And the Raven, never flitting, still is sitting, *still* is sitting
On the pallid bust of Pallas just above my chamber door;
And his eyes have all the seeming of a demon's that is
dreaming,
And the lamp-light o'er him streaming throws his shadow on
the floor;
And my soul from out that shadow that lies floating on the floor
Shall be lifted—nevermore!

The Philosophy of Bird Watching

Introduction: Binocular Vision

I came late to bird watching.

Birdwatching began one early spring when my wife, already an enthusiastic hobby ornithologist, took me to visit RSPB Minsmere. This is a wonderful, wild, and whispering place on the Suffolk coast, where water meets reeds and where time slows to the pace of the fluttering of wings. I borrowed a pair of binoculars to support my wife's eagerness and followed her cue while enjoying the serenity of the landscape. I was unsure what I was looking for and would have been happy to see one of the few birds I recognised, a crow, flying around.

My wife, Larissa, pointed out a marsh harrier gliding low over the wetlands, its long, controlled wings brushing the silence as it searched for food. In that moment, something opened within me that took me back to a childhood experience that I couldn't describe back then. Today, I would describe this moment as a second way of seeing and a new kind of listening.

That was the beginning of this wondrous hobby, which I still get as much pleasure from today as I did back then.

When I'm not bird watching, I live in Bremen, Germany, where I've been for over two decades. The landscapes differ from those in my hometown of York, UK. Here, there is more river than sea, and there are more rooks than redshanks, but the pull is the same. My wife, who has been watching birds for years, welcomed this new chapter in my life with quiet and knowing patience for what I was going through. Nowadays, we walk together more slowly, speaking less at times as we carry thermoses and binoculars, with a growing sense that these avian encounters are never just about the birds.

This book is a philosophical weaving of threads, part memoir, part meditation, and part field notes from the edges of human experience. It is a hybrid work, like the marshes where I first watched those beautiful birds. It is a liminal space, which is neither land nor sea, but something in between. Here, philosophy walks alongside psychology, and both are hand in hand with nature's wonder.

Here, you will find essays on solitude and attention, as well as on beauty and belonging. You will find personal stories, small moments with goldfinches and swans, with still mornings and sudden flights. You will find questions that do not always resolve, along with reflections that bend back on themselves like the curve of a heron's neck.

Why birds and why now? Because in their presence, there is something of the natural world that becomes legible again. Because birds ask nothing of us, yet they remind us who we are when we are not trying to be something. It is in the act of watching them that not only the eye is sharpened, but the soul from which we come.

With this binocular vision, which combines the views of two lenses into one, we begin to see the world anew, not only through clarity but also through depth, contrast, and convergence. Bird watching, for me, is no longer just a practice of looking out. It has become a way of looking in.

Welcome.

The Mindful Watcher

Bird Watching as Meditation: Being Fully Present

There is a moment, just before the bird lands, when the air shifts. A pause in the rhythm of leaves, a silence that settles like mist over the field. If you are truly present, you feel it before you see it. Bird watching begins not with the eye but with the stillness behind it.

This chapter is a meditation on presence. On how bird watching becomes, almost without effort, a form of mindfulness. To stand in a garden or lean against a tree in a city park and watch without expectation and distraction is to inhabit time differently. It is a surrender to what is.

The practice of watching birds requires a kind of attention that is both alert and relaxed. Too tense, and you miss the moment. Too passive, and the moment passes through you. The birds are indifferent to your longing, such that they arrive when they arrive, and you can do nothing other than wait. And in this quiet uncertainty, something shifts inside us.

Much like traditional meditation, bird watching aligns the watcher with the present. The breath slows, thoughts thin to nothingness, and the world becomes more textured, more alive. A robin hopping along the frost-covered grass becomes an entire event. A blackbird's song at dusk is a kind of benediction. The watcher watches and, in doing so, is watched by the world in return.

Psychological Insights: Stress Reduction, Mindfulness, and Attention

Scientific studies are increasingly affirming what many birdwatchers have long known intuitively: that observing birds is beneficial for the mind. It lowers stress levels, improves mood, and sharpens focus. These aren't just poetic claims but measurable effects. A study published in *BioScience* found that individuals living near bird-rich areas reported higher levels of mental well-being. Another study linked even brief exposure to birdsong with reduced anxiety and depression.

Why is this?

Part of the answer lies in attention. In a world dominated by fragmented focus, where screens clamour for our constant engagement, bird-watching is an antidote. It trains the mind toward a softer, more sustained gaze. It teaches patience.

There is also the question of unpredictability. Unlike television or social media feeds, which are engineered to stimulate and satisfy, bird watching offers no guarantees. A kingfisher may flash by in seconds or not appear at all. This gentle unpredictability mirrors life itself and teaches us to hold our expectations lightly.

The psychological benefits of bird watching extend to grounding and embodiment practices. Standing outdoors, breathing in the cool morning air and hearing the rustle of feathers and wind through the trees, is to return to the body. Stress resides in both the past and the future. Bird-watching draws us into the now.

A Personal Transformation: Slowness, Ageing, and Shared Presence

Since beginning bird watching, whether it's from our balcony, nearby parks or in reserves, I've noticed something else start to change inside me; it was subtle yet profound. My bird recognition has steadily improved, though I'm still working on sounds. What was once an occasional curiosity has evolved into a gentle discipline, grounded in rhythm and a way of seeing.

My wife and I used to walk the breathtaking hills of the Lake District in the UK together, taking in the fresh air, the stunning views, and the vast space. These days, the hills are more challenging for me, such that my knees feel the incline more than they used to. While she would set off on small walks to scout local birds, I often found a café and a book (there's always one in my bag). But something began to change when we visited RSPB Minsmere several years ago. There, we walked side by side again, with binoculars in hand. We shared sightings, swapped notes, and pointed things out to each other like old friends discovering something new. She became my coach, gently naming the birds I was seeing for the first time, adding details, and encouraging me to learn on my own.

And then, one day, it happened: I spotted an egret. A flash of white above the reeds. I called it before she did. That moment of recognition was like the striking of a bell inside me. Something opened up. It wasn't just a bird; it was *my* bird. The one I saw, I knew. I felt the thrill of presence, the joy of getting it right. It was, unexpectedly, addictive.

And even more unexpectedly, bird watching did something that not even reading, my lifelong sanctuary, could always do: it stilled my thoughts about work and other distractions, placing me in the moment. The birds were not worrying about deadlines or anxieties. They were there. And somehow, I was there with them. I've come to realise how much time we waste on things that pull us away from the moment. Watching birds reminds me of the value of time well used. And it's deepened the time I spend with my wife, too. Even when we're sitting at opposite ends of a hide, scanning reeds for an invisible bittern, we're together in a new and gentle way.

Philosophical Perspectives: Zen Buddhism, Stoicism, and the Art of Letting Go

Bird watching has, for many, a spiritual texture. It echoes the principles of Zen Buddhism and Stoicism, two philosophies that, though distinct, share an emphasis on presence, acceptance, and harmony with the natural world.

Zen teaches the art of just sitting, *shikantaza*. Just sitting, breathing, and just being. Similarly, bird watching is often just about watching. There is no achievement and no progress to be made. The bird is not a trophy, but a moment of awareness. Zen also speaks of *kensho*, seeing into one's true nature. Perhaps bird watching, too, is a kind of *kensho*: a fleeting glimpse of ourselves in the quiet of the world. When the watcher becomes part of the landscape, without clinging or striving, clarity arises, not as something found, but as something remembered.

There is a story in the Zen tradition of a monk who reached enlightenment not during a sermon or meditation, but when he heard a bird singing just outside the temple wall. The song pierced his thoughts. He stopped thinking and began listening. That's the quiet miracle of bird watching offers: that moment when the mind steps aside, and presence steps in.

Stoicism, meanwhile, teaches us to distinguish between what is within our control and what is not. The bird's appearance is not within our control, but our readiness to observe that it is. Our openness, our patience, our composure; these are within us. A Stoic watcher does not lament the empty feeder. She waits calmly or returns tomorrow.

There is something deeply Stoic in scanning the sky with no promise of a sighting. It trains a muscle we seldom use: the acceptance of reality as it is. The bird may not come. The light may fade. Our feet may ache. But what we bring to the watching, the spirit in which we wait, can still be peaceful, still be whole.

The Roman philosopher Epictetus once said, *"Make the best use of what is in your power, and take the rest as it happens."* Bird watchers know this truth intimately. Some days are abundant. Others are quiet. Both offer a kind of grace.

Both Zen and Stoicism remind us that peace lies not in possession, but in perspective. The bird does not belong to us. The joy lies in watching it go.
Bird watching teaches us the art of letting go, not only of the bird, but of the need to hold the moment too tightly. We observe. We

breathe. We thank the bird for coming. And when it disappears, we remain.

Practical Anecdotes: Pigeons, Beavers, and Beauty in the Everyday

My wife is always on the lookout for a new bird she hasn't seen before. She's often playfully disappointed when it turns out to be another pigeon. Don't get me wrong, pigeons are fascinating in their own right. They're everywhere, and so plentiful it's almost a miracle when one isn't around. But I've grown fond of them with their wind-rattled acrobatics, the iridescent shimmer of their necks catching the light like oil on water, the way they clumsily fumble for water on our balcony with awkward grace. Something is charming about their antics, something humble in the way they exist so abundantly that they're overlooked.

Sometimes, when I slow down enough to watch them, I see stories unfold. One pigeon landing with a stutter-step on the railing, with its eyes darting toward a companion across the courtyard. Another is soaked with rain, shaking out its feathers in a fountain, like a scruffy philosopher. They remind me that even the ordinary carries layers. Even the common can be worthy of reverence.

And then there are the unexpected gifts. Sometimes, we set out in search of a duck or grebe at a pond, and instead, we find beavers: real, live beavers, not ten minutes from home. The first time I saw one, I was stunned. There was no announcement, no rustle or splash. Just a sleek shape gliding silently across the water, with its eyes gleaming and tail trailing like a slow brushstroke. Such quiet majesty, those glossy eyes and broad tails sliding through the water like old poetry.

We stood frozen, whispering to each other like children who had stumbled into a secret world. Since then, whenever they appear, they command my full attention. The birds vanish into the background noise when the beavers arrive, my gaze shifts, and my body stills. I had never seen a beaver before that moment.

21

Now I seek them out as earnestly as any rare bird.

They remind me that the world is more than we expect. That beauty often appears when you are looking for something else entirely. And most of all, they remind me that even when birds aren't around, the watcher's gift remains: to see the world more fully, more tenderly, and more alive.

Voices from Other Watchers

Bird watching is never a solitary act, even when we're alone. All around the world, people raise their binoculars or pause in their tracks to observe a feathered life that is not their own. The following voices offer glimpses into those quiet worlds and remind us how deeply personal, and yet universally human, the watching can be.

Claudia, 52, from Berlin, said: *"I watch birds because they remind me how little I need to be happy. A blackcap in the hedge is enough."*

She described how, early in the mornings in her small urban garden, she would sit with a cup of coffee and wait for the hedgerow to stir. The moment the blackcap appeared, its soft grey body and the little soot-coloured cap, she felt an inexplicable peace. *"It's not grand,"* she said, *"but in that moment, I need nothing more. It's like grace in bird form."* Watching became her ritual, that quiet, daily devotion to simplicity and presence. On this day, her blackcap didn't always show, but even the waiting felt sacred.

James, 34, from Glasgow, shared something more primal: *"My most memorable sighting? A pair of oystercatchers flying low over the sea in Scotland. It was raining. I was crying. I think we were all calling to something larger."*

He had just left a job and was feeling lost, so he decided to take a solitary walk along the coast. The wind lashed against his coat, mixing with the salt and rain. Then the two birds appeared; long-billed and black and white, cutting across the slate grey sea with cries that pierced the noise of the waves. *"I felt like they knew I was there,"* he said. *"Not to comfort me, but to acknowledge me."* Their presence became a mirror, echoing his longing for movement, clarity, and freedom. *"I'll never forget them,"* he added. *"It was like they were drawing a line across the sky, and I chose to follow it."*

Annette, 71, from Yorkshire, found solace in birds during a season of grief. *"I started watching birds after my husband passed away. The quiet helped me grieve. And now, they feel like company. Not always friendly, but always present."*

She spoke of robins that visited her fence each day, and how she began to recognise the subtle differences between individuals. *"They were never trying to make me feel better,"* she said. *"They were just there. And so was I. That helped."* Over time, her grief didn't fade, but it softened. The birds became a rhythm in her life, a way to move forward without letting go. *"It's a comfort to know something will still sing when I wake up,"* she told me. *"Even on days when I can't."*

And Harun, 29, living in Bremen, captured the philosophical spirit of birding in a single sentence: *"Every bird is a mystery solved and a question asked."* I love that.

To him, watching birds is an ongoing puzzle. The flash of wings behind trees, the stillness of a silhouette high on a rooftop, the calls whose meanings remain half-unknown. *"It makes me feel like part scientist, part poet,"* he added. *"Like I'm translating something old and silent."* He described the joy of filling the margins of a field guide with scribbled notes and how each species becomes a doorway to a more profound curiosity. *"Birds make me want to ask better questions,"* he said. *"About the world and myself."*

Each of these voices brings us closer to the heart of what it means to be a mindful watcher, that is, of not seeking, but to receive, not to master, but to meet.

A Field Meditation

Find a bench, a tree, a place where your body can rest.
Leave your phone in your pocket. Let your hands be empty.
Close your eyes for a minute. Feel your breath without trying to change it.
Listen to the ambient sound, the wind, traffic, leaves, and footsteps.
Now, open your eyes.
Choose a point in the landscape, not a bird, just a branch or patch of sky.
Wait. Let your gaze soften. Notice shapes, colours, and shadows.
If a bird appears, welcome it. If not, welcome the silence.
Stay as long as you like.
Five minutes.
Fifty.
When you leave, stroll. You are still watching.

Reflections and Continuations

Don't you find there are seasons to bird watching, literally and internally, and each one teaches us something new? For example, in winter, the sparseness reveals structure, showing that the trees have become maps of memory, so that even the slightest flicker of feathers stands out against the cold air. Yet, in spring, the world begins to overflow again, with warblers and swallows arriving in a wonderful chaos and colour that echoes the urgency of new beginnings. Then summer slows the rhythm somewhat, and the birds retreat into leaves, leaving us to learn to be patient again.

Finally, autumn, my favourite time of the year, brings back the movement of migration, reminding us that nothing remains the same.

Each season offers not just new species, but also a new way of being. In this world of nature and birds, we must adapt to them, and in doing so, we quietly begin to change ourselves.

There's also something worth exploring in the difference between rural and urban bird watching. While nature reserves and national parks offer variety and surprise, I find that some of the most impactful lessons we experience are closer to home. A balcony feeder that brings in the locals like a flitting blue tit and a blackbird that sings after it has eaten. A city tree that attracts a mix of birds that are suited to the environment, like sparrows, blackbirds, and, of course, pigeons.

Or maybe we get a chance to see and hear a gull balancing on a streetlight, proud and white, ready to steal something from a passerby. These everyday sightings carry their own weight in natural pleasure within a constructed, often concrete environment. In these moments, we learn not just to seek beauty in wildness, but to find the wildness in the familiar, which gives us that little connection back to nature. City birds live with us, yet they can remind us of a rhythm that is entirely different to our own.

Of course, not every outing yields a sighting, and not every identification is correct. I've mistaken a thrush for a starling, misjudged a hawk's silhouette, and, frustratingly, I have spent long minutes staring at a leaf, trying to work out what bird it is. And yet, in those moments, something nevertheless softens within. In that moment, we let go of knowing, and we are brought back to a state of humility. And sometimes, in those rare moments, the bird we didn't expect arrives when we stop trying to find it.

This chapter has reflected on many encounters we can relate to, but the truth lies not just in watching the birds; it's in what is revealed when we watch them. It reminds us of how we live in our constructed cities and the societal expectations that govern our lives. Additionally, it's about how we listen, what we yearn for, and what we are willing to wait for. In the end, the birds will do what they've always done: be in the moment and fly on. But for that short while, we were there, they were still, silent and attentive, and we were absorbed in a part of their lives.

And that is enough.

Before we move on, I have realised that another thought has begun to emerge from the shared silence between species. These creatures we watch, these flashes and flickers of a particular feather, are more than just passing curiosities; they are companions of a quieter kind. We don't walk with them in the way we walk with friends, side by side, yet they walk with us differently. They help shape our attention, which gives us our stillness, and in turn, allows us to find our way of being within our part of the world.

To watch a bird is to share a moment with something fully alive and fully itself. And when we do that often enough, we begin to carry that quality within ourselves.

And this is where the next story begins in the slow unfolding of a relationship, not just with nature as a whole, but with its companions who teach us how to belong to it.

A Skyward Gaze

Introduction

I recall that before I became interested in ornithology, the first time I watched a bird soar into the air was a moment when I felt something decisive shift within me. It was a late autumn afternoon, several years before my teens, and the sun slanted low, casting gold across the fields, painting everything in long shadows tinged with a gentle illusion of fire. A red kite (I think it was) circled above the hedgerows. I stood still with my shoes pressing into the damp grass and watched it draw a wide, looping arc across the sky. It barely moved its wings as it rode the currents effortlessly.

There was a strange ache in my chest of longing to be able to distance myself or fly away from the things that were bothering me to wherever I wanted, which was anywhere but where I was at that young age. Something within me recognised that this bird had something I had been searching for until I found what I was looking for forty years later. It was as though the bird had revealed something to me; it was something primal about being alive, and that to live fully is not only to survive or endure, but to rise when one is down and to play with the invisible forces that move through the world. What I now understand, having not understood it in those younger years, is that one must risk falling so that one might fly freely again.

Even now, after my 'aha' moment, I still catch myself tilting my head upward at the sound of wings overhead. I look for birds not just to name them, but to feel that primal freedom again and remind myself that I, albeit subconsciously, have done so to find my new home. It raises a question I continue to ask: What if? What if life could be lived more freely, more lightly? What if we, too, could loosen the weight of all that keeps us earthbound? This is something I still aspire to when I find myself being pulled down by those unseen undercurrents, to reorient myself and find my newer, finely tuned freedom again.

This chapter begins with that question.

Flight has long been a metaphor for inner freedom, transformation and transcendence. It appears in our myths, our religions, and in our dreams. Birds haunt our poems and guide our meditations, as seen in the dark and melancholic poem *"The Raven"* by Edgar Allan Poe (found at the beginning of this book), where the refrain *"Nevermore"* is repeatedly spoken by the mysterious raven.

We envy birds not just for their physical ability to take off from the ground. Instead, we envy them for what they seem to embody in a human life untethered from the gravity of expectation, obligation, and fear. Yet perhaps birds are not merely metaphors.

Maybe they are mirrors to our inner soul.

As I found out after watching that red kite as a teenager is that every time I watch a bird is my confrontation of the possibility that life could be different and that we might move through the world with less friction that would allow us to release our inherited societal burdens, such that we might be able to live more by instinct than by societal rule with more rhythm than schedule. Birds do not ask for permission to be who they are, and they do not apologise for their wildness. Instead, they inhabit their place in the world, fully, vividly, and without explanation.

And so, we look upward. Not only to escape the burdens of our own lives, but to remember that within us, too, is something aerial, primal and free. It reminds us that there is something within that yearns to stretch beyond the narrow confines of our roles, routines, and reputations. There is something within that cries out against the burden of being domesticated.

This is a chapter about that something.

Yet, there is more, something that reflects on the human condition seen and felt through the wingbeats of a kestrel, the migration of a tern, and the silent glide of an owl at dusk. It is about the philosophical recognition of potential freedom and its accompanied lightness. And that is the paradox of flight: that to rise truly, one must often first let go.

And it begins, as many things do, with a single gaze cast skyward to see what we have reawakened and what we have forgotten to feel.

The Symbol of Flight

From the beginning of human consciousness, flight has signified something more than just motion. Long before we built machines to slice through the skies, we dreamt of leaving the earth behind. Across cultures and centuries, the image of the bird appears not just as a biological fact but also as a spiritual and symbolic figure alive with meaning.

Take the myth of Icarus, who fashioned wings of wax and feathers under the guidance of his father, Daedalus. He flew, intoxicated by the thrill of ascent, until he rose too close to the sun. His wings melted, and he fell to his death. The story is often told as a warning against hubris, but there is another reading: one in which Icarus is the hero, not the fool. He was the one who dared. The one who touched a freedom so pure the world could not contain it.

In religious iconography, angels are often depicted with wings as a symbol of their divine proximity. They are messengers between the earthly and the eternal. The winged being is not merely a creature of air; instead, it is a creature of vision, of access, and of liberation from the limits of the flesh. In many indigenous traditions, birds are revered as sacred intermediaries who communicate with the gods, carry prayers to the heavens, and teach us to see the world from broader perspectives.

Flight becomes, again and again, the symbol of transcendence. Even in our dreams, we fly not just for escape, but for transformation. Psychologists from Freud to Jung noted the recurrence of flight in the unconscious. For Freud, flight was a form of wish-fulfilment, a release from repressed tensions. For Jung, it was archetypal in that it manifested our desire to become more than we are. In either case, the motif repeats itself to fly is to access some deeper part of the self, some truth buried beneath the surface of waking life.

Flight is not only mythic or psychological; it is also political. In the modern world, to fly is to cross borders and defy gravity, allowing us to rewrite the script of limitations. Consider how many of our greatest political speeches evoke the metaphor of flight. Martin Luther King Jr. declared, *"Free at last!"*, a cry of legal liberation and spiritual release. The phrase itself encourages our emotions to soar when we hear it, as though it is winged.

To be grounded, in our language, is often synonymous with being punished. Children are grounded when they misbehave and are restricted from accessing the outside world. In contrast, rising above and transcending allows us to take off and be celebrated, as they speak of power, possibility, and perspective.

And yet, there is something more subtle beneath all this metaphor. Birds do not fly to make statements. They do not fly to prove anything. They fly because it is in their nature. It's because the air calls them, and because their bodies are made for motion. There is something profoundly moving in that simplicity because there is no agenda and no performance. It is just being who one is in this moment, for what it is.

This is perhaps why we find birds so captivating. They move through space in ways we can only imagine, and they do so with elegance and with precision, all with a knowing we cannot comprehend. They remind us that freedom is not always dramatic. Sometimes it is quiet. And sometimes it is simply the absence of resistance.

I remember watching a swallow dart through the beams of an old barn, twisting and turning with a joy that seemed to border on play. Yet, there was no audience, and no reason beyond the movement itself. That, to me, is the heart of the symbol. That is the flight as presence. It is not the desire to escape, but the ability to be fully here and in the now.

And yet we return to this symbol again and again because it is needed. Because we, too, want to inhabit a life that moves. We want to feel ourselves in motion, physically and existentially. We want to know that we can change and that we are not forever stuck in the same place with the same identity and the same set of fears.

The bird gives us this hope by teaching us to listen to the wind.

Existential Desire for Liberation

To want to fly is not just to want to move; it is to want to be free. But freedom, as every serious thinker has noted, is not simple. It is not always light, nor is it always joyous. Sometimes it is heavy. Sometimes it is terrifying. Sometimes it is the one thing we fear the most, even though we long for it with every fibre of our being.

Existentialism, more than any other philosophical tradition, wrestled directly with this paradox. The bird, soaring above the landscape, becomes a figure through which we might understand our struggle not to fly in the literal sense, but to exist authentically in a world that often demands conformity, obedience, or escape.

Nietzsche: The Eagle and the Will to Power

Friedrich Nietzsche wrote of birds often as emblems of a higher kind of life. In *Thus Spoke Zarathustra*, he gave us the eagle and the serpent, such that these were companions to the overman, the *Übermensch*, the human who dares to transcend inherited values and create his own life.

The eagle, for Nietzsche, was sharp-eyed, solitary, and a regal, active symbol of freedom. He associated this bird with the will to power of that inner force driving all life to expand itself, to overcome adversity, and to affirm itself in its place within the world. True freedom, in Nietzsche's view, is not safety. It is a risk. It is saying *"yes"* to life in all its difficulty, to becoming what one is, even at a significant cost.

"Man is a rope stretched between the animal and the Overman," he wrote. The rope hangs over an abyss, and yet, the bird flies above the abyss. It does not walk the rope. It defies the ground entirely. Perhaps Nietzsche saw something in that, that the image of life is not just surviving the void, but transcending it.

To watch a bird in flight, especially a raptor, is to see something like that will to power made visible. It does not ask permission. It does not apologise for its hunger or hesitate before the wind. It simply moves.

And so, we look to birds as symbols of freedom and as models that fit our desires unapologetically.

Sartre: Radical Freedom and Bad Faith

If Nietzsche called us to soar, Jean-Paul Sartre reminded us of the cost. In *Being and Nothingness*, Sartre proposed that we are *"condemned to be free"*, a phrase both liberating and dreadful. For Sartre, there is no essential self, no divine plan, and no fixed nature to retreat into. We are what we choose to be, and in every moment, we must choose. There is no escape.

This radical freedom carries a heavy burden of responsibility. Sartre observed that many people attempt to avoid this burden by slipping into what he called *"bad faith,"* living in self-deception, and pretending that the roles or labels that define us are what others perceive us to be.

32

Birds, one suspects, know nothing of bad faith. A swallow is a swallow. A heron does not perform heron-ness; it simply lives it. In contrast, humans often disown their freedom. We hide behind identities, inherited beliefs, and behavioural patterns, relying on repetition to create consistency, which helps define ourselves in specific ways for the benefit of others. All while we neglect our roots and desires of who we are. We forget that we, too, can change direction mid-flight.

Watching a bird adjust its wings in response to the wind or an object reveals an immediacy and responsiveness we often lack. It makes no excuses. It does not say, *"This is who I am, I cannot turn."* It simply turns and gets on with life again.

What if we lived like that? What if freedom were not just a philosophical idea but a daily practice, a way of moving through the world with awareness and accountability?

Sartre would argue that it already is. The question is only whether we embrace it.

Camus: The Absurd and the Flight That Is Not Escape

Albert Camus, perhaps the most poetic of the existentialists, interestingly saw freedom not as transcendence, but as defiance. In *The Myth of Sisyphus*, he gave us a man condemned to roll a boulder up a hill for all eternity and called himself free. Why? Because he refuses to lie to himself. He sees the absurdity of life, its lack of inherent meaning, and he still chooses to act.

Birds, Camus might say, are not free because they fly, and yet, they are free because they fly, knowing that nothing lasts. Their migration may span thousands of miles. They may follow the stars or their instincts, but without guarantee. At some point, storms come, predators wait, and yet they fly.

This, for Camus, is freedom: not escaping the absurd, but embracing it and rising anyway.

I think of gulls we see in a storm; they are buffeted, flung around, and flail as they remain persistent. They do not wait for calm skies. They move through chaos. They find the air currents hidden in the disorder. And somehow, they survive.

For Camus, the absurd is not a reason to despair, but a call to clarity. When we stop looking for the ultimate meaning, we begin to live life for what it is at this moment. Like birds, we stop needing to justify ourselves. We are.

And perhaps that is the most liberating thing of all.

The Existential Bird: A Mirror for Us

Each of these thinkers, Nietzsche, Sartre, and Camus, points us toward a different aspect of freedom, highlighting our inner power, the responsibility we bear for ourselves, and the defiance to carry on regardless of what comes our way. Each of these qualities of freedom reminds us that to be human is not merely to be alive, but to be *aware* of our aliveness and to act within that awareness.

The bird, as a metaphor, serves as a shortcut in relating to that concept because it captures, in a single image, what philosophy takes pages to express.

But more than that, the bird is not just a symbol. It is a living being. It teaches through presence, not through argument. It reminds us that freedom is not always found in thought, but in action, in movement, in instinct, and in the willingness to leap into uncertainty.

Perhaps this is why we go birdwatching. We catalogue what we see to remember to admire and to learn something new about them. When we consider a kestrel hovering above the field, it is not thinking about its freedom. It is expressing it.

We, too, might learn to do the same.

Inspiring Stories from the Avian World

Not all birds are eagles, and not all symbols of freedom are lofty. Sometimes inspiration lies not in the dramatic, but in the ordinary miracles that quietly and persistently unfold across thousands of miles every year. In this section, we leave the realm of abstraction and follow real birds whose lives and journeys offer new ways to understand freedom as endurance, intuition, and a commitment to motion rather than fantasies and societal expectations.

The Arctic Tern: A Life of Light

The Arctic tern is a small, elegant seabird that is both graceful and unassuming. What makes it astonishing is that its annual migration involves flying from its Arctic breeding grounds to the Antarctic and back again. This is a round trip of roughly 70,000 kilometres! No other creature on earth experiences more daylight in a year than this beautiful bird.

There is something almost metaphysical about living a life drawn towards light, over and over, year after year, guided by instinct, wind, and an inner compass that we cannot fully comprehend.

To watch a tern dip and rise over grey northern seas is to see something ancient at work, more impressive than any maps or technology we have developed. It reminds us that freedom does not always mean escape; sometimes it means returning again and again to what calls you, no matter how far. Remarkably, there is a kind of devotion, a rhythm, and a dance with the elements that sets this creature apart from the rest by not avoiding the hardship of travel. Instead, it embraces it. That is its freedom.

What might it mean, for us, to follow our version of light? What does it mean to accept the long journey as part of our nature, rather than as a burden? What does it give the tern that does not question its path? Instead, it gets on with it.

The Swift: Motion without Rest

The common swift is another small, dark bird that is often mistaken for a swallow. Here, the swift has a claim to something almost mythic because once it leaves the nest, it can remain airborne for up to ten months and in that time, it eats, sleeps, and even mates on the wing. It lives in the sky in a way that we can scarcely imagine.

For us human beings, our rest is sacred. We build homes and routines around the need to have that pause. But the swift teaches us a different kind of wisdom, and that is that movement can be rest, too. That to be in flight does not necessarily mean restlessness; it can also mean alignment.

Swifts ride the thermals with such grace that their motion seems effortless. They do not fight the wind. Instead, they yield to it. Where resistance is futile, precision and flow work functions effortlessly. And while they are in the flow, they appear not to rush, and yet they are darting all over the place.

I think of the times I've felt trapped by indecision, by inertia, or by the illusion that I had to stop before I could move again. However, the swift has helped me to think otherwise; that constant motion is a peaceful companion that can help find clarity by staying aloft rather than standing still.

The Marsh Harrier: Presence in the Sky

One spring morning near the coastal reeds, I watched two marsh harriers spiralling in silence. They did not rush, their wings moving with a measured rhythm, sweeping through the air as if they were feeling it by simply inhabiting it. What I witnessed wasn't a hunt, nor even a courtship, but a kind of perceptual attunement to its environment with the bodies moving through space as though it had become a part of it.

Marsh harriers are not dramatic birds. Their dark brown feathers and narrow cream markings are muted and functional. They fly low, skim landscapes while barely disturbing what lies beneath. And yet, when they rise together, they reveal something of an elemental relationship over the sky.

There is a philosophy in their motion, and when we observe them, it is not of a conquest, but of an encounter. Merleau-Ponty once wrote that we do not merely *see* the world, but are in it *through* our bodies. These harriers seemed to understand that long before we gave it words. Their flight is not an escape.

It is not displayed. It is in its purest form.

To watch them was to remember that elevation is not always an escape. Sometimes it is the most grounded act of all as a way of dwelling in the world, not above it but *with* it, in fluid motion, in felt presence and silent knowing.

The Peregrine Falcon: Speed as Surrender

Then there is the peregrine falcon, often called the fastest animal on Earth. In its hunting dive, it can reach speeds of over 300 kilometres per hour. Watching a peregrine stoop, fold its wings, and plunge is to witness something both terrifying and sublime.

There is no hesitation in that dive. No calculation. Only the commitment to motion. The peregrine teaches us that freedom is not always gentle. Sometimes it is fierce and focused, making it a dangerous predator to its prey. Sometimes it involves a risk so committed that there is no room for doubt.

And yet, there is no panic in a falcon's stoop, except for its surrender to gravity that feeds off its instincts as it remains in the moment. It does not dive blindly, but with exquisite control. It knows the limits of its body, and within those limits, it is unlimited.

The lesson here is not that we must move fast or fall hard. It is often the case that freedom requires a leap of faith. Sometimes, the higher the commitment to faith, the faster we move.

Personal Encounters: The Birds Who Change Us

There are also some smaller, quieter stories, of those that happen not in documentaries or migration maps, but in the everyday spaces where humans and birds intersect.

I remember a robin that returned each morning to my windowsill during a long, cold and dark winter. I began to watch him because he reminded me that life was still moving, even when I wasn't. His non-dramatic and straightforward presence felt like a gentle reassurance that even doing the small things without question can take us to the next level of freedom.

Another time, while walking alone during a period of personal grief, I encountered a jay with its flash of blue, its rough, screechy voice, and the way it stared back at me from a distance that felt like a visitation. Not a message, but a moment of that rare and fragile feeling of being part of the world again.

We each have these stories. They are not really about birdwatching; instead, they are about symbolic recognition. About the sudden awareness that something outside of us carries an inner truth, an inner truth we've forgotten, such that our small-feathered friends might understand freedom better than we do, just by living it. In contrast, we read, philosophise, and debate what it is, taking us further away from what we yearn for.

Grounded Yet Longing

We are not birds. We cannot rise on thermals or sleep on the wind. We live with gravity in our bones, burdens in our hearts and are bound to an emotionless system. Yet the longing for flight remains quiet, insistent, and sometimes painful. It vibrates beneath our daily lives, beneath the routines we perform and the walls we build. It shows up in daydreams, in sudden urges to leave, in the ache we feel when watching something take wing.

We are grounded, but not without desire.

There is something deeply human in this tension. We long to be free, but we fear the cost. We want the open sky, but we build structures to feel safe. We crave change, but cling to the familiar. We imagine ourselves as adventurers, but we live as archivists, preserving, protecting, and holding on to the past.

The bird reminds us that we've left our nature behind. Perhaps we've always been aware of this disloyalty and desertion to nature, and because we haven't yet fully experienced it, we can't fully accept it. And in that inexperienced gap between knowing and becoming, between earth and air, there grow the feelings of restlessness. A kind of homesickness for a life we've never quite had.

I have felt this most acutely in built-up towns and cities, where places are full of life, yet strangely heavy, as if brick and concrete anchor everything together, stopping us from seeing further into nature. The roads tell you where you can and cannot go. Schedules dictate your movement. Even leisure is often curated, purchased, and packaged for us to choose from. And yet, above it all, the sky remains, should we decide to look up. It is open and unclaimed, with birds flitting through it without concern for lanes or limits.

In those moments waiting at traffic lights, standing in a queue, or walking with my head down, making sure I don't stumble over a kerbstone (I can't look at my mobile when walking because I tend to walk into someone or stumble over my own feet!), I've looked up and seen a gull drifting high above the buildings. And for a brief second, I remembered something I hadn't realised I'd forgotten, and that life is broader than this. There is always another way to navigate the world.

And yet, here we stay. We nest. We settle. And we remain where we are. I guess there is beauty in that security, too.

Not all freedom comes from flight. Sometimes it comes from finding the stillness within, from choosing where we root ourselves and why. The grounded life is not inherently a lesser one; it is simply different. A wren, after all, is no less a bird for choosing the hedgerow over the sky.

However, the longing remains. Even in those who have chosen stillness, you will find freedom. It doesn't matter whether it is a flicker in the eye when a plane lifts off, a pause when geese fly overhead, or a sudden intake of breath at the sound of wings flapping by.

This longing is not a weakness, nor is it dissatisfaction. It is part of what makes us human. We have become a species that builds a permanent nest and dreams of escape, one that writes poems about flying while planting gardens, and who fear falling but still climb.

The poet Rainer Maria Rilke once wrote, *"The birds fly unaware, yet we are full of flight."* We are full of it even when our feet are on the ground.

And perhaps this is where the deeper kind of flight begins, not in the sky, but in our imagination, by the refusal to be defined entirely by our conditions, in the ability to move inwardly, and even when outward movement is impossible.

The bird sings not because it has answers, but it sings because it cannot help but express the life within it. And so too, we write, we create, and we search for that longing. Our wings may be invisible, but our desire lifts us. Our yearning gives shape to our direction, and sometimes, in listening to that longing, we discover new ways to be free, even here and even now.

Ultimately, we are creatures of paradox. Rooted and rising. Grounded yet longing. Bound by gravity, yet full of sky.

And maybe that's enough.

Flight and Mortality

To speak of flight as freedom is to risk forgetting its fragility.

The bird in flight seems immortal for that moment, and may seem beyond reach, and beyond time, even. But this is an illusion. Perhaps that's why the image moves us so deeply. Because we know, even as we watch, how brief and precarious that freedom truly is.

Birds live close to death when there is a shift in the wind, a missed branch, or a pane of glass mistaken for open sky, and these are enough to end a life. And yet, they still rise. Each day, again and again, they lift off knowing what the earth can take from them. This is not naivety. It is courage. Or perhaps, more simply, it is a necessity. Flight is what they are made for, even when the world is dangerous.

For humans, freedom often comes with a sense of fear. We hesitate before big decisions. We weigh every risk. And we avoid the unknown. And underneath it all, there is often the same quiet terror: what if I fall? What if this costs too much?

But the bird does not live by that calculation. It does not ask whether freedom is safe. It lives in the tension between grace and risk. And this, too, is what makes it a mirror for our condition, for we are not promised safety. We are not guaranteed success. All we have is the ability to choose, to act, to leap and the awareness that our time is limited.

Mortality is not the opposite of freedom. It is its companion.

There is a tenderness to this. Watching an old blackbird limp across a garden path, or finding a feather on the forest floor, we are reminded that even the sky cannot protect us forever. But perhaps this is what makes flight so precious. Not its endurance, but its ephemerality. The very fact that it ends.

The philosopher Martin Heidegger called humans *"beings-toward-death."* Our understanding of mortality profoundly influences our entire experience of being. It infuses our freedom with urgency. With weight. To fly, in this sense, is not to escape death, but it is to live fully in its presence. To refuse paralysis. To answer finitude with motion.

There is, too, the cruelty of how we treat the wildness we admire. We cage birds to keep them near. We shoot them for sport. We fill the skies with wires, lights, and noise. Our longing for flight is often accompanied by an impulse to control it as if the freedom of others reminds us too sharply of our compromises.

But every time we see a bird and feel that surge of awe, we are touching something vital. Something unbroken. And perhaps, through that recognition, we can begin to mourn the parts of ourselves we have suppressed for too long.

I once came upon a dead barn owl that was still beautiful in death. Its feathers were untouched; its eyes were closed, as if it were asleep. It had struck a roadside post at night, perhaps during the hunt, or maybe it had turned too late. I buried it beneath a tree and sat there for a while, wondering what it had seen before the end. Wondering how many nights it had crossed the fields, silent and unseen, alive in ways I could barely imagine.

Flight does not save us from death. But it teaches us how to meet life with open wings.

Personal Reflections: On Seeking Freedom

When I was younger, I used to think that freedom was a destination, some distant place I could reach if I just made the right decisions, packed the right bag, and left behind the right people. And that I have done, moving from one town or city to the next, and even moving to another country, because I imagined it as a clean break, like a beginning with no backstory. It wasn't.

I was running from myself. I know that now.

But freedom, I've come to learn, is through experience, which is rarely a place. It's a way of moving through life. I realise now that it's not in the escape itself, but in how we relate to what we cannot escape. It's in the pauses, the refusals, and the quiet rebellions that happen when nobody is watching.

Still, I've had my fair share of flights. Some are literal, while others are internal, and each has left its mark.

One such moment happened on a cliff edge at Bempton Cliffs. I had hiked alone that day, seeking solitude in the salt and wind. Below me, gulls and gannets circled the sea. I sat down on the grass and watched them move, not toward something, but with something. With the wind, with the currents, and with the world itself. There was no effort in their motion as they went with the flow, giving the feeling of belonging.

I realised then how much of my life had been about struggle. About proving, reaching, correcting and about being someone, becoming someone and escaping someone. But those birds, there was no becoming, only being.

That day marked a step toward no longer needing to earn my place in the world. I felt it as a given. Not because I was special, but because I existed. That, I think, was one of my first authentic tastes of inner freedom.

And yet, the feeling didn't last. Freedom isn't a permanent state. It returns, like breath. Sometimes shallow, sometimes deep. And sometimes we must go looking for it, building on it until it gradually becomes a part of us.

I've also known the mental cage and how it slowly tightened around me and restricting me in my thoughts and behaviours.

43

I've felt it in relationships that asked me to shrink. In jobs that rewarded performance but punished honesty. And the thoughts I had against myself that held me back. That inner voice that said, *"Don't say that. Don't do that. Don't risk that. You're not worth it."*

Today, that voice is rarely longer there. I have a new one who is at peace and looks out for me when that other voice occasionally pipes up. When it does, it's mostly reasonable, thanks to my natural inner voice, which helps us understand and work together. It wants you to be careful, to be liked, and to be safe, but if we tell it otherwise, it gradually begins to believe it. But over time, if left unchallenged and loved, it builds a nest inside your chest, protects or warns you and calls it home.

I recall a moment, years later, sitting at a dinner table with people I once called friends, laughing on cue, nodding at all the right moments, and feeling utterly absent from my own life, like a bird watching itself in a cage. That moment didn't appear to be a crisis. It seemed to fit into others' expectations. And that was the problem.

Freedom, I've learned, often starts with discomfort. With the uneasy recognition that something isn't right. That the life you've constructed no longer fits the person you're becoming.

So, what do we do?

We begin small. With choices. With questions. And with the truth. We listen to the inner shifts, the stir of restlessness, and the whispers of other ways and options. We do not have wings, but we have instincts. We have imagination. And we can refuse to move and to change course if we don't want to.

Sometimes I think of freedom as a mental migration. Not one long arc, but a series of short inner flights taking us from fear to courage, from silence to expression or from shame to self-acceptance. And like the Arctic tern, we return to mental and physical places we thought we'd left behind, only to see and feel about them differently, which allows us to inhabit them anew.

There are also moments of flight we experience every day.

It could be due to a deep conversation that sheds an old skin, or a song that makes you forget the time. Perhaps it's something as simple as walking barefoot across wet grass, in saying no or saying yes. Or it could be when we walk away, or conversely, when we come home.

It's in those simplest acts of integrity that we reclaim that space within ourselves.

And in those rare moments when freedom floods the body, when we dance, when we laugh so hard we forget our name, and when we fall in love without armour, is when we are reminded that we were made for this. Not just for survival, but for aliveness and being in the present and for the freedom of movement and motion.

Even now, when the sky darkens with doubt and when the world seems tighter than ever, I go looking for birds with my binoculars in hand, with complete attention and reverence for what I am about to experience. And this is done with the hope that they'll remind me of what I so often forget that I, too, can rise. The cage is not locked. It never was, only we thought it was. To believe it is closed, our spirit can only wait for me to notice how open it is.

We may never fly like swallows or falcons. But we can live like them in truth, in rhythm, and motion, so our spirit and soul can fly like swans and falcons. We can choose to stop resisting the wind and start moving with it. It's our conscious decision we need to make.

That is our version of flight.

And it's enough.

A Sky Without End

And so, we return to the sky.

I don't mean the sky of postcards or weather reports that I want to turn to; I want to turn to the sky as a horizon. And, I suppose, as a metaphor to reflect something like a mirror when we begin to consider the endless field of things that can become possible again, that allows thought to dissolve into presence and where longing doesn't ache anymore, that enables it to soar.

The sky doesn't explain itself because it doesn't need to. It simply holds everything together, allowing it to do its things with wings and wind, storms and stillness, all with the glint of feathers and the fall of light. And in doing so, it becomes the space in which we imagine ourselves freer, more expansive, and more alive.

Birds know this instinctively. They trust in space, in currents, and in the invisible scaffolding surrounding the air. They do not know where they will land, yet they continue to move.

Perhaps that is the most profound lesson of all.
To live as if we, too, can move without knowing.
To act with courage, since nothing is certain.
To stretch the limits of what our lives have become by flight rather than force gives us the freedom we have been searching for.

Nietzsche once wrote, *"You must be ready to burn yourself in your own flame; how could you rise anew if you have not first become ashes?"* Here, we find an invitation that freedom is not always a matter of lightness. It is sometimes on fire.

But what remains, when all is said and sung, is the sky.

It asks for nothing.

Yet, it offers everything.

And somewhere within us, beneath the roles we play, the fears we face and the careful lives we juggle, it is essential to remember that we are not strangers in this vastness. That we, too, are made with some parts of the sky.

All we have to do is look up to make that connection.

The Aesthetics of Bird Watching

The Gasp of Beauty

It happened so quickly, I almost missed it. A flash of emerald and fire across the surface of the lake; it was there and then, in an instant, it was gone. I stood motionless, not quite believing what I'd seen. Then it returned, arcing out from the shadows beneath the willow: a stunning kingfisher! It hovered for a split second, long enough to catch the shimmer of its wings in the early morning light. Then it plunged like a jewel dropped into the water.

There was no one else around to see it, and I had no binoculars in my hand as I had just arrived on my bike. I wasn't prepared, and they are so quick that if you are not ready, they don't wait. Nevertheless, I had a sudden rush of astonishment, joy, and awe at having glimpsed it for that brief second. And beneath it all, rose a strange and quiet grief, a grief that I could not hold the moment, that it was already over even as it happened, and I didn't see another kingfisher again that day.

This is the kind of beauty bird watchers know well: not the kind you expect to see or seek out easily, but the kind that arrives unannounced. Yet, when it comes, it affects and rearranges something inside you that remains for a lifetime. When such a bird appears, it isn't just a bird in the field of vision; it is an event, a happening to be cherished, and a visitation we have been honoured to take part in.

To observe birds is to be repeatedly caught off guard by their beauty. You scan a hedgerow and find goldfinches feeding among the thistles. You glance up and see a heron gliding across a pink evening sky. And if you sit by a lake and a grebe surfaces so close you can hear its breath. These encounters don't announce themselves with fanfare because they slip quietly into your awareness that lingers as a collection of impressions imprinted onto our memory.

It's not only the rare or colourful birds that provoke this reaction. Sometimes, it's the sheer stillness of a dunnock in the undergrowth, the flicker of a wren's tail, or the way a flock of starlings move as one fluid body across the dusk. Bird watching doesn't have to be dramatic. It is, more often, subtle little things that impress us and within that subtlety lies a profound kind of emotional wonder.

What we feel in these moments is sometimes challenging to put into words, the mere aesthetic pleasure or biological curiosity they give. And then there is something deeper, a kind of sacred attentiveness that we rarely experience in our daily routines. It is a sense that, for that moment, the world has lifted its veil and revealed something pure and true. And you have been chosen, not for who you are, but simply for being there.

Bird watching, then, is more than a hobby. It is a practice of attention. And it is a way of participating in beauty without needing to possess it. It teaches patience, humility, and presence. It rewards stillness. And it honours the slow miracle of simply looking.

And this is what this chapter is about: looking.

It is about beauty as a force, which we can find in art galleries and cathedrals, as well as in the reeds in the wings and the morning light. It is about what birds offer us beyond identification or rarity: the chance to feel awe, an opportunity to remember that we, too, are part of something wild and radiant. And sometimes, it is to stand still and watch, that is the most honest way of saying 'thank you.'

Beauty in the Wild

There is a kind of elegance in the wild that no artist can fully replicate, no algorithm can predict, and no composition can improve upon. It is the elegance of a bird in its natural element. Yes, there is the flash of colour or the arc of a flight as individual aspects, and there is how everything fits together. The environment, the movement, and the moment all coalesce into something that transcends design. It is beauty, wild, and it is unscripted, all in one.

Birds have long captivated the human eye due to their unique movements. A swallow skims close across the water. A redstart fans its bi-coloured tail with a flick. A crane rises slowly, with control and elegance as the sunrise breaks. These behaviours are gestures of natural forms of grace.

Even the most common birds are works of art when seen with attention, like the iridescent neck of a pigeon when the sunlight reveals the greens and purples that most people never stop to notice, like the subtle browns of a female chaffinch that echo the colour of autumn leaves. The more you watch, the more you realise that the birds are the decoration. They are nature's brushstrokes, constantly moving through the frame of time.

Colour is, of course, one of the most immediate sources of delight, ranging from the sudden burst of blue from a Eurasian jay's wing to the crimson flare of a tanager in the tropics, from the strange contrast of a puffin's beak of orange, black, and cream in geometric perfection to the simple curved red beak of a chough. These evolutionary signals are also a form of aesthetic phenomenon. They take our breath away because they break our rhythm by surprise.

Along with colour, bird watching is about its form, motion, and texture, like the long silhouette of a heron standing motionless in a marsh or the swift arc of a kestrel as it dives. And then there is the flickering movements of a goldcrest among pine needles. Each is a scene in a play that has no script and no encore. All it has is presence.

Then there is the song.

There is the nightingale's liquid notes that sing in the dark, the melancholic repetition of the cuckoo somewhere in a wood. Let's not forget the buzz and click of warblers and the haunting boom of a bittern. Birdsong carries more than sound; it carries the season and mood, creating a lasting memory. For many, it is the first sign of spring. For others, a reminder of places loved and lost.

Beauty also lives in patterns: the V-formation of migrating geese, the undulating movement of starlings in murmuration, or the sudden lift of a flock of lapwings as if responding to an invisible cue that seems to hold a form of choreography within them. Instead, there is a unity without control and a fluidity without command. This is participation at its finest.

What bird watching teaches us, perhaps more than anything else, is that beauty does not always need to be framed, and it does not need to be rare or permanent. All it needs is to be noticed, like the sparrow singing on the fence post or the blackbird hopping on the lawn, where each moment becomes an aesthetic revelation, if we allow ourselves to look.

Some of the most profound beauties in bird watching are seasonal. I love the sudden return of the swifts in early summer as they scream through the streets like living commas in the sky and the calm arrival of waxwings in winter, with their silky crests and dusky masks lending a quiet drama to bare trees. Just as I enjoy (and still do) going brambling with that scent of cold air while trying not to slice my fingers on those thorns. Each appearance is like an ever-changing brushstroke on nature's never-ending canvas, reminding us that time is moving and that you are part of it.

Don't you find that, unlike museum art, the beauty of birds does not stand still? It constantly changes as the moment passes, slipping into the shadows and eventually disappearing behind a hedge or across a hill. And it is in that impermanence that lies a different kind of beauty that must be met with attention, gratitude, and grace. The beauty of birds can only be witnessed for what it presents to us.

To observe a bird in the wild is to be reminded, which we can often forget, that the world is not solely human. That there are other rhythms, other priorities, and other forms of meaning that are unfolding all around us, too. And it is that these have their own music, elegance, and astonishing beauty, which we experience by being in the present, with open eyes and ears.

Philosophical Reflections on Aesthetics

Birdwatching is rarely discussed in philosophical texts. However, I think it should be. Because to honestly watch a bird by attending to its form, its movement, and its unexpected arrival is to experience something close to what philosophers have tried to name for centuries: aesthetic judgement, the sublime, and the beautiful.

Let us begin with Immanuel Kant, whose *Critique of Judgement* laid the groundwork for much of modern aesthetics. For Kant, beauty is that which pleases 'disinterestedly', meaning we find something beautiful not because it serves us or satisfies a desire, but because of the form itself. It gives us pleasure simply through its appearance, without needing to be useful or owned.

When I stand still and watch a bullfinch perched in the early morning frost, I do not want to possess it, and I do not wish to change it because I take great delight in its presence. That, for Kant, is disinterested pleasure. And it is at the heart of aesthetic experience.

Kant also distinguished between the *beautiful* and the *sublime*. While the beautiful is harmonious, proportioned, and gentle, the sublime overwhelms us. It is a vast, powerful, and sometimes even frightening experience. Think of a murmuration of starlings at dusk, where thousands move as one. Or think of a sea eagle wheeling above a northern fjord. Or maybe the silence after a sudden lift of birds, the way the air holds the echo of their wings. These moments astonish us. They point to something beyond comprehension. And that, too, is an aesthetic experience of the sublime kind.

In the presence of such moments, we are not merely seeing. We *feel seen*. We feel small, yet also part of something greater. Then there are those boundaries of the self that blur, even if only for a second. We are no longer the observer and become the observed, caught in a web of meaning far older than our language can ever describe.

Arthur Schopenhauer, writing in the 19th century, took a different path and, interestingly, arrived at a similar place. In *The World as Will and Representation*, he describes aesthetic experience as a temporary liberation from the *'will'*, that restless, desiring force that drives all life. Most of the time, we live caught in the grip of wanting food, safety, love, and validation. But in these beautiful moments of pure aesthetic contemplation, we forget ourselves completely through the power of observation.

Schopenhauer writes: *"In the moment of aesthetic perception, we are no longer individual will-driven beings, but pure subjects of knowledge."* This, I believe, is what happens when we watch a bird without naming it, judging it, or taking its picture. It's when we allow ourselves to *be with it*, without an agenda.

The bird, in that moment, becomes more than a species or a specimen. It becomes a portal into another being. And we, by observing it, participate in that being without trying to alter it. At first, I thought this was being passive. It isn't. It is being attentive. It is, in Schopenhauer's terms, *a moment of philosophical grace.*

I also find that there is something democratic in bird watching that aligns with this aesthetic philosophy. Unlike a museum, which may be expensive or exclusive, nature is available to all. Even a robin sitting on a garden fence, singing its beautiful song, can offer as much aesthetic experience as a Renoir, and to a kestrel hovering above a motorway is no less sublime than a new Gothic cathedral. In this way, bird watching fulfils the promise that philosophers have often longed for, and that is the possibility of beauty that is both universal and unowned.

Let's turn to consider Edmund Burke's early thoughts on the sublime. In *A Philosophical Enquiry into the Origin of Our Ideas of the Sublime and Beautiful* (1757), he argues that the sublime evokes awe, and even terror, because it confronts us with magnitude and power. Watching a raptor dive at full speed or hearing the eerie, distant cry of a loon across a lake at night are not comfortable experiences, yet they move us within. They awaken something more profound than pleasure, like a trembling kind of reverence that takes us back to our primal instincts.

And then there is Maurice Merleau-Ponty, the 20th-century phenomenologist, who adds yet another layer. He focused on how we perceive it, rather than the content. For Merleau-Ponty, perception is never neutral. He said it is embodied and relational because we participate in nature. The world is not out there for us to examine like an object; it is a living entity that *includes* us.

When we watch a bird, we might think we are standing apart from nature, looking in. We are involved. Our body, breath, and presence all shape the experience. Perhaps we have noticed that a blackbird's call sounds different when we are calm compared to when we are anxious. A lark's rise affects us differently at dawn than it does at dusk. That's our perception of what is going on, which is lived and is not calculated.

This should matter to us because it means beauty is not an object but an event that occurs between the bird and the observer, a form of dialogue that does not need words.

And here, perhaps, we approach the spiritual dimension of aesthetic experience. I want to say spiritual in a doctrinal sense, but it's not. It is in the sense of an encounter, where something within us opens up toward something outside of us; this is where perception becomes reverence.

Bird watching, then, is more than recreational. It is philosophical. It asks us to see without consuming, which allows us to witness our observations without needing to master anything special. It reminds us that beauty is a relationship rather than a commodity.

And that to engage with such beauty is not to meet it in its freedom. Possession taints it.

What philosophers have long struggled to name is the moment when the self or the ego drops away and when presence overtakes purpose. It's when awe stuns us into silence that birds offer freely and daily, if we only learn to look.

Psychological Perspectives: Why Beauty Moves Us

What happens inside us when we witness something beautiful? Why does the flash of a kingfisher, or the shimmer of a hummingbird's throat, stir such disproportionate joy? Psychology, unlike philosophy, doesn't seek to define beauty in the abstract; it studies its effects. And the findings are striking.

Research into awe and aesthetic emotion reveals that when we experience moments of natural beauty, especially unexpected ones, they can trigger measurable changes in our nervous system. They slow our heart rate. They regulate breathing. And they increase parasympathetic activity. This is the system responsible for calm, recovery, and the repair of the body and mind. In short, beauty heals.

This is not a metaphor. Studies at the University of California, Berkeley, and elsewhere have shown that experiences of awe, a close cousin of beauty, increase generosity, decrease inflammation, and help reduce self-focus. The mere act of gazing at a vast mountain, a sunset, or a murmuration of starlings can reframe our perspective, shifting us away from the micro-anxieties of daily life and toward something larger.

Psychologist Dacher Keltner refers to awe as the 'small self' experience. When we feel awe, the ego shrinks. We become more connected to others, more open, and more attuned to the present moment. Bird watching, particularly when practised attentively, provides a near-ideal setting for these effects. It slows the mind. It requires stillness. And when beauty appears, like a sudden movement in the trees or a rare colour against the grass, it strikes like grace.

There's also the element of surprise. Our brains are wired to respond to the unexpected. When something breaks a pattern, especially in a delightful way, it triggers the release of dopamine, creating a sense of reward and pleasure. This may explain why so many bird watchers report a rush of joy when they see a new species or witness unusual behaviour. The mind loves novelty, but the heart loves wonder. And Bird watching offers both.

Then there's the psychological concept of *mindfulness*, which is increasingly recognised as a therapeutic tool. Mindfulness is, in essence, the act of paying attention on purpose, in the present moment, without judgment. Bird watching demands just that. To truly see a bird, you must be quiet, listen, and observe not only the bird but also the environment, including the light, shadows, and even the wind. It is mindfulness in motion.

Many clinicians now recommend bird watching or 'green time' as part of mental health recovery, especially for those dealing with anxiety, depression, or burnout. The reason is simple because beauty grounds us. It draws us out of rumination and into a relationship with it. It connects us to something we did not create and cannot control.

There is also the role of emotional identification. We see ourselves in birds. In their fragility. In their movement. And in their song. A robin singing at dusk evokes not just admiration, but empathy. A storm-blown osprey struggling against headwinds might mirror our private battles. And beauty moves us because it reveals us to ourselves, both gently and painfully.

And let's not forget memory.

Beauty, especially when encountered outdoors, tends to become deeply ingrained in our memory. A flash of yellow may, years later, evoke the exact moment you saw your first golden oriole, and a particular birdsong might transport you to the place where you first felt truly at peace. These memories are visceral, tied to breath, to smell, and to mood. They form part of what psychologists call *episodic memory*, which is a personal, emotional, and enduring form of memory.

For those who have suffered trauma or chronic stress, beauty can provide a reparative function. It doesn't erase pain, but it does offer an alternative kind of moment within. One that says: *There is still wonder in the world. There is still softness.*

Psychologists have also explored the concept of *frisson*, a sudden, fleeting thrill often accompanied by goose bumps. While most commonly associated with music, it can also be triggered by a sight or sensation that evokes a profoundly emotional response. Seeing a rare bird, especially in an unexpected location, can certainly evoke a frisson, like a pang in the chest, a breath held longer than necessary, or a sense that something significant has just happened.

And then there is the most elusive yet powerful element of all: connection. Birds do not know us, yet we feel they meet us. We don't converse with each other, and yet something is exchanged. Maybe it's a glance, a call, or a moment shared. These small encounters with the wild spark a profound psychological response, which causes us to feel a sense of belonging to life.

In a world increasingly mediated by screens, algorithms, and artificial noise, beauty offers an unmediated moment of genuine connection, a point of authentic reality. Bird watching, in particular, reminds us that the world is not something to be optimised or controlled as we are brought up to believe, but something to be encountered.

And that, in itself, may be the most significant psychological gift of beauty because it invites us to *stop striving* and start seeing.

Encounters with the Extraordinary

It begins, often, as a flicker. A shape in the periphery or a shadow that moves wrong. And then it clarifies itself into a burst of impossible colour, or a silhouette too rare to be imagined, and then your heart stutters, which causes you to catch your breath. And you know, in that moment, that you are seeing something truly extraordinary.

Bird watching is built on ordinary moments, such as robins in the hedge and sparrows on a wire. But every so often, the world lifts its veil to offer a glimpse of the miraculous. These are the encounters we remember for the rest of our lives. They do not just delight us. They alter us. Permanently.

The Resplendent Quetzal: Myth in Motion

In the highland cloud forests of Central America lives one of the world's most revered birds: the resplendent quetzal. It is sacred to the Maya and Aztec civilisations, and it was seen as a symbol of the gods because it was so beautiful and otherworldly that to kill one was to invite spiritual punishment. Today, it remains an emblem of Guatemala and a living myth.

Seeing a quetzal in the wild is no easy task, as the forests are dense, and the bird is shy. But when it appears, it *glows*. Its iridescent green plumage with a scarlet breast, and tail feathers that stream behind like ribbons of air. It doesn't seem possible, and yet there it is.

What strikes most observers is not only the colour, but its softness. The quetzal doesn't shout its presence. It's as though it floats through the trees, almost too slowly, as if it were suspended on a different kind of time. Watching it, you feel as if you're trespassing on something sacred.

That is the essence of the extraordinary. It reveals itself, but only partially. It leaves us with more questions than answers and with reverence, even if we don't understand it.

The Shoebill: Stillness as Presence

Ah, now to one of my favourite non-native birds that captured me like no other when I saw it for the first time at a bird park in Germany.

At the other end of the spectrum, that is less delicate and more prehistoric, is the shoebill. Native to the wetlands of central Africa, this bird looks like something from another era. Its beak is massive, like a sculptor's tool, and its stare is unrelenting and unlike many other birds, because it doesn't flit or flutter. It stands with outstanding patience, which can last from minutes to hours.

There is a kind of philosophical shock in encountering the shoebill because it challenges our assumptions about beauty. This is not a bird designed to charm. It is intended to *be*. And in its immobility lies a strange power; you feel yourself being watched, measured, judged, perhaps, and yet, without any malice, there is pure presence.

The shoebill reminds us that beauty is not always elegance. It is not always colour or song. Sometimes it is the quiet refusal to move. To be still in a world obsessed with motion, that is, inhabiting space without apology.

The Mandarin Duck: When Beauty Escapes Expectation

Sometimes, the extraordinary appears where it doesn't belong. Such was the case in 2018 when a mandarin duck turned up in New York's Central Park. For days, the city buzzed with crowds gathering, taking picture after picture, all because this is not a native species. This was a bird of East Asian origin, likely an escapee from captivity. But that didn't matter.

What mattered was the sheer extravagance of the thing with its deep russet cheeks and cream crown. Then there were its impossibly ornate wings, standing like sails at rest. It resembled a painting, with its parody of beauty. And yet, it was real, and it was *in New York.*

This duck reminded people, amid the urban noise and pace, that there is still room for astonishment. That even in the most constructed of environments, the wild can intervene, beauty can cross oceans, and such wonders can drop in, uninvited.

Something is humbling in that.

We often go in search of the extraordinary on distant mountains and in remote jungles, yet sometimes it finds us, perhaps on a lunch break or during a walk in the park on a grey Wednesday afternoon.

Personal Sightings: When Time Stands Still

I remember the first time I saw a waxwing.

I was walking through a car park on a dull winter morning, not expecting anything. And then I heard it, a high, electric trill. I looked up and saw a small group of birds on a bare rowan tree, feeding on the last red berries. They were soft grey and cinnamon, with flashes of yellow and red on their wings, and that unmistakable crest like a 1950s jazz musician. They looked tropical and misplaced, like they had flown out of a dream.

I stood in the cold, watching them for what felt like hours. Nobody else noticed. It was just me and the birds and the quiet snow beginning to fall. And I felt, inexplicably, *alive.*

Another time, a friend of mine travelled to Scotland's west coast in spring, hoping to see puffins. After a long and wet hike, she reached a cliff edge, and there they were. Dozens of them, waddling across the rocks like tiny, clown-faced monks. Their orange feet with their sad eyes and their comical dignity. She laughed aloud, but it wasn't in mockery, she told me. It was in joy and gratitude.

These moments are not just memories. They are markers. They remind us of who we were at the time, what we needed, what we feared, and what we hoped. The birds didn't care about any of that, of course. But in watching them, we get to re-meet ourselves.

Why the Extraordinary Matters

We live in a world that increasingly confuses the extraordinary with the sensational. But the kind of beauty that birds offer is not always grand. What it is, is intimate, and when it happens, it happens in seconds. It does not try to impress. It's just *the way it is*.

That is why these encounters matter so deeply to us. They reorient us. They remind us that not everything can be planned, bought, or repeated. That some things are still wild, still unowned and still capable of surprising even the most jaded among us.

They teach us that the world is more enchanted than we think and that we, too, are part of that enchantment. Isn't that wonderful?

To see an extraordinary bird is to feel the mystery of life condensed into feathers and flight. And in that brief encounter, we glimpse something of our longing: to witness beauty and be touched by it.

Attention as Devotion

To watch a bird is, in the end, an act of love.

Not sentimental love. Not the love that clings or claims. But a quieter love, one that is a form of reverence. It is a way of saying, *You matter*, simply by paying attention.

In a world that runs on distraction, attention becomes a radical gesture. It is the opposite of control and consumption. It is not about capturing an image or adding a species to a list. It is about being presence in accepting the world on its terms.

Bird watching, during this spiritual practice, doesn't necessarily lead to answers, but it does lead to a particular presence within us, and it is that part of us that reminds us of our roots. It trains the eyes to see what is often missed in everyday occurrences. And what I love is that it invites the heart to open to reality. One minute, you are alone in a field, the next, you are sharing that field with a creature older, wilder, and more precise being of anything you could have invented.

It's that type of encounter that matters.

Because every act of attention is also an act of humility, we sometimes stop assuming that we are the centre of our world. We begin to see ourselves as part of a larger, living tapestry that sings, migrates, dances, and then dies. And yet, when we notice it, it changes us forever.

There is a phrase I often return to: *what you attend to grows*. If we attend to beauty, we will find more of it. Likewise, if we view a childhood wonder through a child's eyes, the world becomes a wondrous adventure again. Attend to the wingbeat, and you may feel your pulse again, and that is what makes us feel alive.

The aesthetics of bird watching involves the whole self. They invite us to admire what we see, and this leads to our inner transformation through the act of *seeing*.

And in that seeing, something sacred stirs within like a robin in winter, a wren in the reeds or a heron lifting at dawn.

This is the world speaking.

And all we have to do is listen.

The Ethics of Bird Watching

A Quiet Responsibility

The first time I realised I might be too close was when I was standing near a hedge at dawn, watching a warbler fidget through brambles. I had been still for some time, wrapped in the hush of morning, totally lost in the intricate movements of that small, feathered life that made me late for work. But then, it stopped singing. It wasn't immediate, but a gradual and uneasy silence settled in the branches. After a few seconds, I stepped back and the bird resumed its song.

That was the moment I understood: watching is not a neutral act. As bird watchers, we speak often of respect, but we rarely explore the ethics of our presence. We carry our cameras, notebooks, optics and other things into habitats that existed long before we arrived. Over time, we tread paths through nesting grounds, we crouch beneath trees and lean over wetlands because we desperately want to see what attracts our attention. And yet, in that wanting, we sometimes cross a line we don't notice until the silence falls.

Ethical bird watching begins with awareness of what we observe and how we observe it. This is not just what we learn on our adventures, but also what we leave behind. The question is how our love for birds can manifest as care rather than harm.

There is a kind of humility that comes with this realisation. To love something truly is to ask what it needs from us, rather than what it can give. The birds do not need our admiration. All they need is habitat, safety and breathing space. What they need are watchers who know when to stay back, when to remain silent, and when to walk away.

This chapter is about that form of care. It is about ethics that are not a set of rules imposed from outside, but rather a way of moving through the world with sensitivity and respect. It is about the choices we make in the field and the forest, at feeders and fence lines, on social media and in scientific logs.

And it begins with a simple idea that beauty demands responsibility.

To watch birds is to be gifted with wonder. But wonder, if it is to mean anything, must lead somewhere, such that it must take shape in joy and conduct through conscious action.

It's not asking for grand, performative action. It's asking for a quiet action, a stepping back and a softer voice with a slower breath. It's asking us to choose not to photograph a nest or to refuse to disclose the exact location of a rare sighting, which aligns with the decision to learn not only the bird's names but also its needs.

These small gestures are not footnotes. They are the ethics we need to abide by.

To be a birdwatcher is to belong to something larger, like a migration of human attention that is moving, ideally, toward protection, preservation, and a deepening respect for our feathered friends and their environment.

The Watcher's Footprint

We enter the field with good intentions, binoculars in hand, and go in search of beauty, awe, and a connection with the natural world. We move softly and speak in whispers, in search of our target as we wait patiently for a key movement in the hedge or reeds. But even the most careful watcher leaves a footprint on the path and the birds themselves.

The ethics of bird watching begin with this fundamental truth: that our presence alters the environment.

Too Close to Comfort

One of the most common forms of unintentional harm is proximity. Sometimes we are too near and linger too long in one spot, or we try to chase a better angle for a glimpse. To us, it may seem harmless, especially when a bird does not immediately take flight. However, many species are masters of concealment, so their silence is not always a sign of comfort; it may be a survival strategy.

Ground-nesting birds, for instance, may sit tight while a human draws near, hoping not to reveal the nest. But its stress levels rise, and if we stay too long or return too frequently, they may abandon the site. Sadly, the price of our curiosity can be the loss of an entire brood.

The solution is simple but not always easy: restraint. We must learn to read the signs: those nervous calls, fidgeting, and unnatural stillness are signs that we need to step back and give them that space, remembering the privilege we have of watching ends when the well-being of the watched begins to be threatened.

Feeding: A Double-Edged Act

Feeding birds is one of the most common ways people connect with wildlife. It offers closeness, regularity and even a kind of intimacy. But it's not without risks.

Yet feeding can create dependency, alter migratory patterns, and, most critically, concentrate birds, thereby facilitating the spread of disease. When hygiene is poor, feeding stations become transmission points for illnesses such as trichomoniasis and avian pox. Moreover, some foods, such as bread, offer little nutritional value and may even do more harm than good.

This does not mean we should never feed birds. However, it does mean we must do so thoughtfully, using clean feeders, appropriate food, and with seasonal awareness. Feeding is not inherently unethical; it is context-dependent, particularly when it serves as a lifeline during a harsh winter and, conversely, poses a heat hazard during late summer with limited water availability.

As ever, the key is knowledge and care.

The Ethics of Photography and Sharing

In the digital age, bird photography has experienced a surge. Zoom lenses bring us so close to details that we once never noticed, like the subtle textures of a nightjar's plumage or the shimmer on a hummingbird's throat. These images inspire and educate us and are to be celebrated. However, if not handled carefully, they also put pressure on nature and its wildlife.

In pursuit of the perfect shot, photographers may disturb sensitive habitats or stake out nests for hours, often unaware of the cumulative stress they inflict on the animals. What begins as a desire to honour beauty can become an intrusion.

And then there's the question of location-sharing. Geotagging rare or nesting birds on social media can inadvertently attract visitors who trample their habitats, disturbing the birds, other creatures, and the environment. Sadly, it can even result in egg theft in some regions. That very visibility we offer birds may work against them.

In such moments, we need to be discreet, sharing wisely, blurring location data, and avoiding revealing sensitive nest sites. Choose storytelling over spectacle and let ethics guide the lens.

Sound, Light and the Unseen Pressures

Yet, our impact is not only physical because birds are acutely attuned to various sounds, such as loud conversations, sudden laughter, or playback recordings used to lure them in, which can disturb their natural behaviour. The use of call playback, in particular, is controversial because it may potentially draw birds away from their nests or disrupt feeding. It is best avoided altogether during the breeding season and always used with caution.

Light, too, disorients birds, such as flash photography at night, torches used to observe nocturnal species, and even light pollution in urban areas. It interferes with their navigation or even alters their daily behaviour. These are quiet harms that are usually unintentional; nevertheless, they are real.

Ethical bird watching means considering not only what we see, but also what we bring with us: light, sound, scent, or energy. It means asking: Does this action serve the bird, or does it serve only me?

Habitat as Home

Finally, we must remember that birds inhabit specific locations and have distinct needs. A hedgerow is not just scenery, and a wetland is not just a photo backdrop. These are their homes, which are fragile and complex, intricately linked to other animals, plants, and the environment.

Even off-path walking can cause damage by trampling wetland plants, disturbing insects, or unintentionally compacting soil in nesting grounds, which may seem like a minor inconvenience for our wonderful hobby. Yet those inconveniences are the ripple effects felt across entire ecosystems.

Some reserves now mark sensitive areas with signs or ropes. However, even in unmarked areas, we must rely on our intuition and knowledge by exercising a sense of shared responsibility. If a spot feels too pristine and delicate, then it probably is, so please walk away and leave it alone.

Ethical bird watching, in this sense, is less about following rules than about cultivating habits, and we can do this by slowing down, by paying attention, and by asking ourselves what kind of footprint we're leaving.

Conclusion: A Lighter Touch

None of this is meant to shame or discourage. On the contrary, it is an invitation to deepen our practice further. To let our love for birds become more than a delight, we must allow it to grow with care.

We will always leave traces, but we can choose to leave fewer by walking with a lighter step, moving with greater awareness, and observing nature's wonders as guests.

And when we do, something changes in the birds and us and for that moment, we become part of the landscape.

Perhaps the most rewarding aspect of bird watching is enjoying the birds in their natural habitat and learning how to coexist with them.

Philosophies of Conservation

The ethics of bird watching rest on a deeper worldview, one that asks not only how we behave but also what kind of beings we believe ourselves to be in relation to the world around us. The moment we shift from seeing nature as a backdrop to seeing it as community and as kin, then everything changes. This is the foundation of conservation, promoting protection through collaboration between science and philosophy.

Aldo Leopold and the "Land Ethic"

In the early 20th century, American ecologist and writer Aldo Leopold proposed what he called a *"land ethic"*. In his influential book *A Sand County Almanack,* Leopold argued that we must expand our sense of moral responsibility beyond the human realm to soils, waters, plants, animals, and to the land itself. *"A thing is right,"* he wrote, *"when it tends to preserve the integrity, stability, and beauty of the biotic community. It is wrong when it tends otherwise."*

This is environmentalism taken one step further, evolving into a more moral perspective.

For bird watchers, Leopold's ethic presents a clear challenge that it is not enough to love birds. We must care for the systems that sustain them. The marsh, the cliff, the thicket and the open sky are not scenery. They are nature's sacred architecture. When we start to protect a habitat, we preserve the *possibility* of birds.

Leopold understood that conservation cannot be enforced from the top down. It must arise from affection, from a personal and emotional bond with the land and its life. Bird watching, in this way, becomes more than recreation. It becomes moral education. We learn, through encounters with what we cannot learn through abstraction, that this life matters.

Moreover, we begin to see ourselves not as observers, but as participants in a living web.

Deep Ecology and the Intrinsic Value of Nature

Building on and deepening these ideas, Norwegian philosopher Arne Næss introduced the concept of *Deep Ecology* in the 1970s. Where traditional *('shallow')* environmentalism often focused on human-centred concerns, such as pollution, resource use, and sustainability. Deep Ecology asked us to abandon anthropocentrism entirely.

According to Næss and those who followed him, nature has value *in itself* rather than solely for human interests. A bird does not need to be beautiful, rare, or valuable to deserve protection. It is enough that it exists. It has its own being, its own right to flourish, regardless of whether it is watched, loved, or even known by us. This is a radical shift.

Many conservation efforts still rely on what some call *"charismatic megafauna"*—the animals that evoke the most public sympathy. But Deep Ecology invites us to go further. We need to extend our care to the unnoticed, the unseen and the unloved, such as the drab sparrow, the plain warbler and the nameless insect that feeds the chicks.

From this perspective, ethical bird watching is about *relationships*. We watch because birds are our neighbours in the shared home of the Earth.

This idea leads to what Næss called *"ecological self-realisation,"* which is a gradual widening of the self to include the non-human world. By becoming participants in ecosystems, we start to blur the line between *"us"* and *"them"*.

From Dominion to Participation

Both Leopold and Deep Ecology challenge a worldview that has dominated Western thought for centuries: that humans stand above or apart from nature. This view, rooted in certain theological and industrial traditions, imagines the earth as a resource, a tool and as a stage.

However, birdwatching counters this idea every time we lift our binoculars, because we learn by witnessing nature at its purest. We are eternal students and should never try to become masters is at the heart of an emerging ecological consciousness. It is about humility, which gives rise to ethics.

Because when we know that our existence is entangled with the lives of others, feathered or otherwise, we begin to act differently. We begin to ask, *"What does this bird need from me?"* and *"Where should I step lightly or not at all?"* along with our usual questions: *"What do I want to see?"* and "Where *can I go?"*

This is philosophy lived at the highest level of habit.

Care as an Aesthetic and Moral Act

There is an aesthetic beauty in this way of thinking. It is to live in proper relation with birds and habitats that is *"good,"* as well as it is beautiful. There is a level of grace and humility in restraint, just as there is elegance in the well-timed withdrawal. And don't you find there is poetry in walking a path without leaving a trace?

Ethical bird watching, then, becomes a form of devotion to contemplative ecology, a way of aligning our gaze with the land's well-being.

We don't have to withdraw from the world or avoid joy. On the contrary, I find it means finding joy in care itself. In knowing that our love for birds protects them, isn't our admiration meant to be a form of honour?

It is easy to romanticise nature and place it on a pedestal, which was a challenge I faced when writing this book. However, after some thought, I believe it is better to say that conservation requires more than admiration, which aligns with the book's theme: it necessitates action, often difficult choices.

And although that may seem disappointing, sometimes it means closing a trail or telling another watcher to step back, even if it means missing out on that beautiful creature or not getting into the ideal position to take that one-in-a-lifetime photo.

But every ethical decision made in the field, however small, becomes a thread in a larger moral tapestry. It stretches from our muddy boots to global movements, from the care of the local park to planetary healing.

We are a part of the birds we watch, just as we are part of the exact nature's system. Their fragility is our own, just as their future is ours, too.

The Ethics Beneath Our Feet

To stand in a meadow and listen for skylarks is to make a choice, whether we move with care or entitlement, and whether we see the land as ours or as something we share.

Aldo Leopold, Arne Næss, and others offer us more than ideas. They offer us new identities and to be moral agents within them. Each time we step back into a wonderful world of beautiful natural intricacies, society continues to push nature further to the ever-receding edges of freedom. This is the invitation of conservation philosophy that we act because we love.

Because birds are not just beautiful:

They are teachers.
They are neighbours.
They are part of us.

Citizen Science and the New Conservationist

For centuries, the role of the scientist and the observer was thought to be separate. Scientists studied the world as its citizens lived in it. However, in recent decades, that boundary has become increasingly blurred, particularly in ornithology. Today, people who watch birds are not just spectators. We are data collectors, map makers and contributors to global research. We are, in the truest sense, *citizen scientists*.

This evolution has altered the ethics of birdwatching by transforming observation from a private pleasure into a public good. It has also reminded us that caring for birds is not only about what we avoid but also about what we give back.

Watching as a Contribution

Bird watchers today play a central role in some of the world's most crucial conservation databases. Platforms like *eBird*, developed by the Cornell Lab of Ornithology, have revolutionised how we track bird populations, migrations, and patterns of decline. Tens of thousands of people log sightings daily, which is feeding an ever-growing reservoir of knowledge that scientists alone could never gather.

These contributions allow researchers to monitor species distribution across vast geographic and temporal scales. They help detect early warnings of habitat loss, climate-related range shifts, and local extinctions. They also provide crucial context for conservation decisions, ranging from land-use policy to protected area design.

When a birder logs a sighting of a curlew in a threatened wetland or makes notes about the absence of nightingales in a region where they once thrived, we are not just keeping a personal record; we are building a collective map of avian life, and we have become a part of the planet's story.

In this way, we, the citizen scientists, bridge two worlds: the emotional intimacy of personal experience and the structural urgency of scientific response.

Examples of Global Initiatives

Beyond eBird, there are numerous initiatives powered by citizen effort:

The British Trust for Ornithology (BTO) engages amateur observers in regular breeding bird surveys, nest recording schemes, and migration watches. Their data underpin nearly all of the UK bird conservation work.

The Audubon Christmas Bird Count, established in 1900, is now the world's longest-running citizen science survey. Every December, volunteers across North America tally birds across thousands of sites. This annual tradition has not only informed ornithology but has also fostered generations of engaged naturalists.

BirdTrack in the UK, **BirdLife International** projects, and **Atlas projects** across Europe and Africa all rely heavily on local watchers. Their reach is as broad as the wings they trace.

Each checklist submitted, each count recorded, is an ethical act, a form of service, and a vote for preservation.

An Ethic of Accuracy and Humility

With this power comes responsibility. The ethics of citizen science mirror those of fieldwork, emphasising precision, honesty, and humility. The problem is that overreporting, misidentifying, or submitting fabricated data can skew findings, leading to misinformation that inaccurately informs policy and, sadly, erodes trust.

What I do like is that ethical citizen science goes beyond accuracy, encouraging a willingness to learn that we are not always right and that we occasionally have to correct our errors and accept uncertainty in our observations. Birding, after all, is full of doubt, even from my experiences in asking myself whether it was a lesser whitethroat I saw or whether I heard two birds or one? Good citizen science is about *care*.

And that care includes the welfare of the birds by avoiding breeding colonies to get a closer look. It also means resisting the urge to *"tick"* a species if it might stress the individual or disrupt its behaviour. It means choosing *ethics over ego*.

The best observers are not those who see the most, but those who see with the most tremendous respect.

From Watcher to Steward

What emerges from all this is a new figure is the *watcher-steward*, someone who views birds as beings to be protected. It is someone who recognises that information is generative, guiding restoration, influencing habitat management, and shaping essential funding decisions.

In this way, bird watching can remain both aesthetic and contemplative while we adhere to a protective civic duty towards them. In other words, we become engaged citizens through quiet activism, grounded in data and care, by investing time in supporting our feathered friends.

What I love about this is that it gives the role, and me, a deep sense of meaning. In a world that often feels fractured and overwhelming, citizen science offers a way to reconnect with nature; it's a way to act locally yet have a global impact, and it's a way to turn attention into action.

Watching birds may seem like a small act in itself, but it can have a profound impact. All these thousands of small acts, when joined together, create systems of knowledge and care that are vast enough to support an entire winged world.

The Science of Belonging

Citizen science is reshaping the story of bird watching. It is no longer just a pastime for solitary contemplation; it has evolved into a shared endeavour that enables us to participate in something much larger than ourselves.

Naturally, it requires discipline, and in return, it offers a sense of belonging to a community of watchers and the birds themselves.

And what greater ethical call could there be than to see more clearly, to record more carefully, and to love more actively while enjoying this wonderful and absorbing hobby?

I once thought that watching birds was a way of retreating from the world, yet now I realise that it is a way of getting closer to nature by helping to repair it.

Stories of Hope: Conservation That Worked

In a world attuned to crisis, it is easy to believe that all is lost. The headlines scream of extinctions, habitat loss, and warming seas. And while this is sadly true, much has been lost, and there is more at risk. If, however, we observe amidst the decline, there are also stories of return, of places healed and of threatened birds reborn, which has been down to the people who chose care over convenience and patience over profit. Stories like these remind us that conservation is a movement and a promise that we can work together to make a difference, whether big or small.

The Osprey's Return to the UK

For much of the 20th century, the osprey was absent from Britain. Once widespread, these fish-hunting raptors had been driven to local extinction by egg theft, persecution, and habitat degradation. By the early 1900s, they had disappeared, silent from the lochs and rivers they once ruled.

Then, in the 1950s, something quiet and astonishing happened. A pair returned to Scotland, unaided, from Scandinavia. It was a tentative moment of hope and fear as volunteers rallied to protect the nest. Watchers set up camp to create a makeshift sanctuary, and the birds began to breed. Because of this and over the decades since their return, the population has steadily grown.

Today, ospreys nest across Scotland and in parts of England and Wales in areas where their absence was once felt permanent.

Their comeback is a triumph of biology, an excellent testament to the patience and collective effort of the wardens who slept in wet tents, the schoolchildren who raised funds for nest platforms, and to the birders who chose stewardship over spectacle.

The osprey's return tells us that loss is not always final, and that presence is a choice we can all support.

Barn Owls and the Power of Nest Boxes

Barn owls, with their ghostly faces and silent flight, have long haunted both myth and meadow. However, by the 1980s, their numbers had declined steeply across much of the UK, primarily due to changes in farming practices, the loss of nesting sites, and the use of rodenticides.

And here enters a simple intervention: the nest box.
They are built by hand, placed in barns, trees, and quiet field edges that are most suitable for the owls. These are wooden structures that offer them what modern agriculture took away: a safe place to breed. The outstanding effect is that over the following decades, thousands of these boxes were erected, often by volunteers, small charities, or farmers themselves, and the impact has been remarkable. In areas with dense networks of boxes, barn owl numbers have stabilised and, in some places, even increased. Local populations that once hovered on the brink of collapse now thrive. And the boxes themselves have become symbols of what is possible when conservation meets community.

What this has taught is that solutions can be simple and shared. Anyone with a toolkit and a ladder can make a difference.

Wetland Restoration and the Return of the Bittern

Bitterns are birds of secrecy. They are herons that haunt reedbeds, which remain often unseen, although their deep booming calls are more often heard than their striped bodies observed, frustratingly! Once common in the fens and wetlands of England, they rapidly became rare by the late 20th century. Drained marshes, industrialised farming, and the creeping silence of ecological neglect caused habitat loss.

And then came the wetland revival.

Conservation bodies, such as the RSPB, began restoring large tracts of wetland by creating reedbeds, managing water levels, and ensuring the proper ecological balance. At first, it was an act of hope more than certainty. Would the birds return?

They did.

Bitterns began to breed again, and the number of booming males, which were once in single digits, has started to increase. Today, the population remains fragile but is gradually recovering. Each spring, the strange, resonant call of the bittern echoes once again through the reeds.

The story of the bittern is a story of time, listening and believing that absence can become presence if we are willing to wait and work.

The California Condor: A Near Resurrection

On the other side of the Atlantic, a far more dramatic rescue unfolded. By the 1980s, the California condor, North America's largest land bird, was down to just 27 individuals. Habitat destruction, lead poisoning, and hunting had decimated its numbers that making extinction seem inevitable.

It was when biologists and conservationists made a controversial decision. They decided to capture every remaining wild condor and brought them into captivity. Critics called it desperation, and it may seem so at first thought. Yet, through intensive breeding, habitat protection, and massive education efforts, the condors have begun to recover.

In the decades since, these birds have been reintroduced into the wild in California, Arizona, Utah, and Baja California. Their numbers are still small, and their future remains uncertain, but for now, they are thriving, breeding, and alive.

The California condor's triumph was, and still is, a complex, costly, and contested decision. What it does prove is that even a species on the very brink of extinction can be pulled back.

Community Conservation in Action: The Swift Tower

Closer to home, another quieter revolution is taking place is the rise of community-led conservation. Let's consider the Swift Tower. It is a tall, specially designed structure placed in urban or semi-urban areas to provide nesting sites for common swifts, whose numbers have also declined sharply due to the loss of traditional buildings and roof spaces.

Across Europe, community groups have installed swift boxes in churches, schools, and homes. Some communities have built full-scale towers. Other groups monitor nests, host festivals, and teach children about these birds, enabling thousands of swifts to nest safely each year in places where they had once been displaced.

The beauty of these projects lies in their grassroots scale, which is accessible and provides hope. There is no large-scale bureaucracy or spending budget interfering with their future. Because of these communal initiatives, we see that we don't need to be scientists to be conservationists. All we need is care and persistence.

Why These Stories Matter

In conservation, hope is often seen as naive. But hope is a refusal to give up. These stories matter because they remind us of what's possible when care becomes action.

They remind us that ethics can scale even the most obstinate issues we have in preserving wildlife.

That a single pair of ospreys, a nest box in a barn, and a restored marsh can ripple outward into ecosystems, economies, and even cultures, those birds, though small and fleeting, can anchor such movements. That love, when disciplined and directed, can reverse decline.

These are not just case studies. They are templates for the future. They show us how to move from grief to response. From beauty to responsibility. From watching to doing.

They do not erase the losses. But they balance the ledger.

They say: *Look. This bird is back because someone cared enough to try.*

Toward an Ethics of Wonder

We began with the quiet act of watching a warbler in a hedge and a shadow on a branch, and now we end with something even more silent: the internal shift that happens when admiration turns into care. This is the heart of ethical bird watching, of a *wonder made responsible.*

Wonder, after all, is where most of us begin. The first bird we ever truly saw, not just looked at, that likely opened something in us. Maybe it was a mental door, a stillness within or a gasp of breath. And once it is opened, that door cannot be closed, and the world is never the same again. Instead, it is more alive where we notice how delicate it is, which makes our ethical outlook more urgent.

Ethics grows from this place within as a devotion to think and question: *What does my love for this bird ask of me?*

It might ask for the distance between us, or it might ask for silence. It might ask us for years of patience, or to allow it its thirty seconds of courage in a moment of need. It might ask us for a donation for a nest box, or for a correction to be shared gently with another watcher. It might ask for nothing at all, but to allow its presence.

But it will ask.

The birds do not ask, of course, and not in any language we understand. They ask through their lives, their migrations, and, sadly, through their soft disappearances, for our attention. It's how we respond that will shape not only their future, but also our own.

Because this is not just about birds.

It is about how we live on this earth, how we view what we do not own, and how we learn to be at peace with what we cannot control. It is about remembering that our gaze carries weight and can become their shelter.

Ethical bird watching is a path that we walk with binoculars in hand, stories in our pockets, and humility under our feet.

And it begins, again and again, with this simple act:
Look, and love, without taking.

A Life Shaped by Watching

A Life Shaped by Watching

One spring in Germany, my wife and I spent time together in and around Bremen. She had been observing birds for some time already, and my enthusiasm was still relatively new; she pointed them out on walks and named them with ease. What began as a newcomer's curiosity about what my wife gained in these moments quickly turned into a ritual of walks, conversations in the hide, and the shared silence as we scanned the trees. The habit with a quiet companionship, deepened by the birds we shared our lives with.

I began to see how bird watching offered *orientation*, a way of being present to return to something essential deep within, and I was starting to notice the world more clearly. And in doing so, I began to feel more like myself.

That's how bird watching enters life as a subtle reordering of attention. For some, it begins with a spectacle, such as a kite in the open sky. For others, it's the rhythm of shared mornings, the slow accumulation of names, songs, and sightings.

This chapter explores the shift in how watching birds becomes an integral part of who we are, shaping our identity, fostering community, and connecting us across time, family, and geography, about *belonging*.

Bird Watching and the Making of a Self

We often define ourselves by what we do, where we're from, or what we believe. But just as important are the quieter aspects, such as the habits that shape our days and the lenses through which we view the world. For many of us, bird watching becomes one of those quiet, defining acts.

When we watch birds regularly, it begins to structure our lives around how we pay attention to them. Over time, we start to notice more than just birds; we see how the light is different, the play of shadows through the seasons, and what I love is the differences in the silence, depending on where I am. When we walk, our pace changes and we begin to tune in differently with our eyes and even how we use and move our bodies. We walk slower, take steps more carefully, and even stop mid-step when we notice something. We listen longer, trying to separate the sounds to detect whether we have heard a warbler amongst the mix. And it's when we take the time to pay attention that we begin to slow down, which allows something within us to align.

In psychological terms, our identity is constantly changing, shaped by our memories, environment, relationships, and repeated behavioural patterns. The more often we engage in something meaningful, the more likely it becomes an integral part of how we perceive ourselves over time. Bird watching works in a similar way, too. We don't wake up one morning and say, *"I am a bird watcher."* Instead, one day we realise and think, *"I see differently now."* The birds have stopped being occasional treats and have become part of how we navigate the world.

Don't you find that there is also something quietly radical about choosing to become an observer? We live in an era of performance where we are encouraged to be visible, productive, and responsive. But as bird watchers, we become something else, becoming more receptive and attuned to what is happening around us, which leads to a patience we once considered foreign. It affirms a version of selfhood that is built on presence and attention. Everything else becomes secondary.

Many people who take up birding later in life describe a kind of homecoming, and I agree with this sentiment. It is as if the world we had once moved through for decades had been layered with meaning we hadn't noticed before. As if birds had been speaking the whole time, and we have finally learned how to listen to them. Such a transformation as this can feel almost existential. Where once a tree was just a tree, now it holds other lives and stories. Over time, we instantly recognise the flash of a redstart or the trill of a wren. We mark the seasons by temperature and by the departure and arrival of birds, such as when the swifts return, the robins start singing, and when the blackcaps have fallen silent. The world has become animated, with specifics, and is alive wherever we look.

And in this aliveness, we begin to view ourselves differently as participants in a shared ecology of awareness, progressing from being *in* the world to being *with* it.

Bird watching can also offer refuge. For introverts, neurodivergent thinkers, or anyone who has struggled with fast-paced or highly social environments, birding provides a space where solitude is a strength. It rewards the stillness, it honours the quietness, and it allows room for the kind of perception that doesn't shout.

It also provides a steady thread in times of personal change, allowing us to notice that relationships shift, our work evolves, and some beliefs deepen or fade. And throughout all this time, the birds continue their cycle of migration, return, singing, and breeding, and even then, they still surprise us. They offer a rhythmic continuity like a wheel that turns, bringing us into our seasons of self.

Over time, bird watching can become a kind of autobiography in fragments. We remember the birds, where we were, and who we were with when we saw them. The first time we saw a kingfisher or the last time we heard a nightingale, and it is in this strange sense of awe that envelops us when we see a bird we cannot name, that we experience the quiet joy when, later, we can identify it. These become more than sightings. They become themselves *in time*.

Some people find themselves in the thrill of the chase by hunting out and seeing rare birds, which involves long drives, patience, and staking out an area. Yet when they have found and identified it, that moment of confirmation washes through us, and nothing else seems to replicate it. Then others find themselves drawn to familiar local areas, such as observing the robin in the garden or the woodpecker hammering away in the old oak. There is no right way to build our identity through birding. What matters is that it offers a frame that gives us a way of living attentively, and of saying: *this is who I am, and because of this, it is what I care to notice.*

Ultimately, bird watching teaches us a profound orientation toward nature and ourselves. It offers us a mirror which is sometimes literal, like in the shining eye of a blackbird that says, "You are here, you are a part of this, *and because of this, you are watching, and you are being watched, too.*"

Belonging in the Flock: Rituals, Groups, and the Social Brain

Bird watching may seem, at first glance, like a solitary activity. A lone figure with binoculars surrounded by the silence and in being with the stillness, while paying attention to our feathered friend. And for many, this hobby begins in this way, which is usually taken further and has always had a social dimension, one that is often deeply felt yet overlooked.

At its heart, birding is a practice that brings people together around a shared type of attention. It offers a rare kind of social interaction that is slow, non-competitive, and again, built on presence. We stand in silence next to someone as we scan the treetops, and somehow, without saying much, a bond forms. We are *watching the same thing and* tuned to the same frequencies.

Psychologists have long noted that shared experiences are among the strongest sources of human connection. In particular, experiences that involve synchrony, such as doing the same thing at the same time, can rapidly create a sense of belonging. This is why music festivals, rituals, and sporting events evoke such a powerful sense of community. Bird watching, although quieter, works in the same way.

In a group bird walk, we move together, we pause together, and we hush at the exact moment when a warbler is heard somewhere in a thicket. We raise our binoculars almost in unison. This bodily synchrony produces an awareness and a sense of *we*. We are here, we are watching, and we are part of something shared.

Birding also develops language. There's a lexicon of calls, slang, and shorthand words like *"a lifer," "dip," "drake," "drumming,"* and *"a twitch."* There are codes of behaviour that speak quietly, opening up the view that gives us time to contemplate. These are our rituals, embedded in culture, that help birders feel a part of something recognisable, even when meeting with strangers.

And then there's the thrill of *joint discovery*. Few things bind people more quickly than the moment of spotting a rare or unexpected bird together. You look at someone else and see in their eyes the same disbelief, the same joy in spotting the barn owl at dusk, the unexpected appearance of a wryneck or the sudden silence that comes when a raptor passes overhead. These moments live longer within us when they are shared.

Group birding also invites a rare kind of generosity, for example, when someone points out a bird you would have otherwise missed, when someone lends you their scope, or when someone quietly identifies the call for you without correction. Birding, at its best, tends to reward mutual noticing, and in this mutual exchange, a new friendship grows.

For newcomers, joining a local bird group can be a gentle yet powerful entry into a new type of community, characterised by pre-dawn meet-ups that lead to shared flasks of coffee and quiet conversations about past sightings and future trips. It's not loud or fast. But it's real. The feeling that you are part of a kind of loose *flock* that is loose, and perhaps, attentive to one another.

Some communities take this even further. Birding festivals draw hundreds or thousands of people together in celebration of shared passion. There are talks, walks, photography exhibitions and citizen science presentations. In these spaces, people with similar interests form a sense of belonging. One can walk into a marquee in the middle of nowhere and immediately feel among one of our own.

And this is intentional. The psychology of belonging is deeply tied to identity. When we share a passion with others, we reinforce our sense of self, which makes us feel safer. Belonging reduces anxiety, increases resilience, and deepens our emotional well-being. Birding groups, especially those that welcome all ages and abilities, offer these benefits quietly, consistently, and in a safe, enthusiastic environment.

The social side of bird watching also exists online. From international Facebook groups to local WhatsApp alert networks, the birding community has become increasingly digital. While some lament the rise of screens in a world meant to be watched through field glasses, others embrace the way digital platforms connect isolated individuals, such that a birder in rural Suffolk can now exchange notes with one in Kerala and young enthusiasts in an urban flat can find mentors, friends, and inspiration without leaving their room.

What these communities share, either online or offline, is a sense of recognition when you mention your favourite bird and someone nods, or you describe the sound of a curlew and someone smiles. Maybe you say something like, *"I think I saw..."* and someone leans closer. This kind of listening is rare in modern life. In birding, it's almost instinctive.

There is also something particularly touching about the shared *rituals* of birding: the early starts, the waiting in the cold and the whispered joy of success. These habits build rhythm into relationships. They mark the seasons in friendship and not just in nature. *"This is when the warblers return." "This is the weekend we go to the estuary."* This is a shared time that birds shape.

And sometimes, it's not the birds that matter the most. It's who you were with when you saw them.
That, perhaps, is the real gift of community in bird watching: not some group imposed from outside or a structure we must

conform to. It's a gathering that forms gently around attention, stillness, and those fantastic stories.

A flock doesn't need to be tightly bound either. It can be scattered or we can go about it alone, yet, even in its looseness, we are always aware of others when the time comes to share.

And that's how many bird watchers come to feel about their community, because a deep and unspoken understanding loosely holds it together. You may not meet often or speak much, but you know you are not alone.

Across Generations: Family and the Inheritance of Wonder

Some passions are passed down in books or heirlooms. Others come in the form of stories, meals, and photo books. And then some slip quietly across generations in the form of shared attention, the pointed fingers, and the simple act of noticing things together. Yet bird watching often enters a life as an inheritance.

For many, the first bird ever truly seen is the one someone else pointed out. A parent saying, *"Look, a blackbird,"* a grandparent lifts the binoculars to your eyes when you were a child, or a sibling tells you to hush because they heard or briefly saw something in the hedge. These are small moments that leave impressions. These are the light footsteps in the soil of memory that deepen over time.

My love for birds grew slowly, and part of what gave it shape was the quiet joy of watching alongside my wife. What began with her pointing out birds on walks and naming them with a soft certainty became a shared rhythm between us. The weekend morning walks gradually became our ritual, and the sighting of a kestrel became a story we still remember and share. These memories, and many more, are the ones we share and remember together.

In this way, bird watching can become a language between people, a shorthand for care, by learning someone's favourite bird and seeing the joy in their face when they hear the first swallows of summer. There have been times when I have driven a little slower through a wooded lane, just in case we get to see the owl again. These acts are small, and they say, *"I see what you love, and I love that you see it."*

Within families, bird watching can become a part of the architecture of relationships. Children get to grow up with feeders outside the window that are regularly visited by tits. They learn to listen for a robin's song. And they inherit the field guides with pencilled notes and margins filled with stars next to their important information. There are the binoculars that once belonged to someone, now no longer here. There are faded photos of trips to the wetlands, filled with memories of holidays where the highlight was a flash of colour in a treetop that didn't even last a second.

In some families, bird watching is passed down explicitly through generations of enthusiastic birders, who maintain dedicated lists, specific birding regions, and migration calendars to catch the last of the leavers and the first of the arrivers. In others, birding is more ambient, with a love of nature that binds to an attentiveness to the outdoors, marked by the regular habit of pausing to look in the direction of a fleeting sound. Either way, it enters the bloodstream.

And for those who didn't grow up with it, bird watching can be something new that becomes old. Something you begin as an adult and then pass on, like when you take your child to the park and find yourself pointing out a heron. You kneel beside your niece or nephew and show them how to trace bird tracks in the mud. You begin birding all over again, only this time, as the guide.

There's also something unique in the way birds accompany family memory. A place where you once saw a linnet as a child becomes meaningful for the rest of your life. A trip to the coast when a seagull shat on your shoulder. A funeral marked by a robin that sat near the ceremony on another gravestone, as if witnessing it. These birds are our memories and are the keepers of our stories.

They also mark generational shifts. The birds your grandparents knew may no longer be common in the area. The species you grew up with may now be rare and endangered, as these too become part of the shared narrative embedded in our shared sightings.

Wonder is a posture we carry within us that needs to be found and nurtured, and bird watching teaches it beautifully through waiting and patience. It teaches us by looking for significance. When this is modelled in families, it becomes a kind of legacy and a new perception.

Even when families are scattered, bird watching can remain a quiet bond. A message with a photo, accompanied by a comment underneath: *"Look what I saw today."* Or as I did for my wife with a new guidebook as a birthday gift. This conversation goes across generations about where the swifts have gone this year. These affirmations show that we still see, care while we are still watching.

Birds, in this way, become the messengers of people and nature, as well as the link between people, connecting the past with the present and passing on what was passed down.

A Global Community of Watchers

Birds have no borders because they cross oceans, continents, and political divisions without visas or any allegiance. They follow the wind, the seasons, and their instinct. They migrate in arcs that defy human cartography. And in doing so, they connect us.

To be a bird watcher is to belong, often unknowingly, to a global fellowship.

We can meet someone in another country, perhaps on a path in a Costa Rican rainforest, or in a hide beside a Scottish loch and find that you share a language of gaze and gesture. Our binoculars are raised, a finger points and a name is whispered in wonder. Then came the exchanged smiles. We may not speak the same language, yet we both know the thrill of recognition: a bird seen *is a bird shared.*

This has happened to me more than once when moments of connection with strangers occur, bridged by the simple act of noticing the same bird. Once, while travelling in England, I stood quietly beside a man in his sixties, both of us watching a marsh harrier glide low over the reeds. We said nothing for several minutes. When the bird vanished into the treeline, he turned to me and smiled. *"Always beautiful,"* he said, with a slight accent. And that was enough.

There's something profoundly reassuring in these encounters. They remind us that bird watching is more than just a hobby; it's a way of relating to the natural world through one another. I find it teaches presence, humility, and shared attention. Those are the values sorely needed in a fragmented age.

And now, in the digital era, this global connection has only grown.

Platforms like eBird and BirdForum enable bird watchers from every continent to share sightings, ask questions, celebrate lifers, and seek help with identification. A birder in São Paulo can upload a photograph of a tanager and receive comments from someone in Bangkok. Someone in Nairobi can enter data that supports conservation decisions in Europe. Data, pictures, and stories all travel as easily as the birds themselves.

These platforms, as they collect information, create relationships, generate trust and form webs of awareness. There are entire forums and subgroups devoted to local patches, urban birding, women in birding, LGBTQ+ birders, and many other topics. The global birding community, while sometimes niche or eccentric, is growing more inclusive and more connected each year.

Citizen science, too, is international, with projects like the Global Big Day. This is an annual celebration where bird watchers around the world submit their checklists on the same day, making it a ritual of joyful contribution. In 2023, over 50,000 people from 200 countries participated in this remarkable event. Each checklist was an act of love and a piece of data. Each watcher became part of something larger.

There are also beautiful examples of bird-watching as a cross-cultural exchange.

In Japan, urban birders celebrate the return of the Japanese bush warbler (*uguisu*) in spring as a symbol of seasonal renewal. In Australia, Aboriginal communities have long incorporated bird knowledge into songlines, stories, and tracking skills. In Colombia, local ecotourism initiatives empower communities to protect endangered species while offering guided walks to international visitors. In Kenya, Maasai rangers now lead birding tours in grasslands that were previously used solely for livestock grazing.

These stories matter. They remind us that bird watching extends beyond a Western pastime and is a global practice with diverse voices. As more people from diverse backgrounds take up binoculars, the birding community itself becomes more diverse, more reflective of the world it seeks to celebrate.

Birds, after all, are found everywhere.

They live in war zones, gardens, deserts, and megacities. They sing in languages that no human knows. And wherever they go, someone is watching and listening to them.

Sometimes, that watching turns into friendship. I've heard stories of people meeting in hides and planning birding trips together for years afterwards. Others have developed pen-pal-style relationships with fellow birders overseas, exchanging bird news, books and even handmade gifts. Some couples met on a birding tour, and others have formed lifelong friendships during guided walks.

There is something about such shared wonders that breaks down barriers and erodes hierarchies. It's incredible to notice that in front of a rare bird, all egos fall silent, and we become watchers.

This global network is also a network of concern.

When a species declines in one country, others take note, which can help inform and support conservation efforts that require collaboration across borders. The spoon-billed sandpiper's future depends on work in Russia, China, Myanmar, and Thailand. The swifts that return to Europe in spring must survive winters in sub-Saharan Africa, and today, the fate of birds is always a shared responsibility.

And through this responsibility, solidarity is created. We may never meet the people protecting wetland rookeries in Peru or monitoring seabird colonies in Iceland, yet we are on the same side and looking in the same direction. In an era of climate crisis, habitat loss, and growing isolation, this sense of global kinship is essential.

Bird watching offers more than sightings. It provides a template for living with attention, humility, and a keen awareness that we are not alone. This way of living extends across borders, carried by birds and cherished by people who care.

We watch locally, and we belong globally.

A Flock of One's Own

Ultimately, bird watching is neither entirely solitary nor entirely social. It lives somewhere in the in-between, a quiet rhythm that shapes us both as individuals and as part of a larger, loosely woven flock.

You might stand alone in a forest with the binoculars to your eyes, watching a treecreeper spiral silently up the bark. Or you might sit in a hide with ten others, all breathing as one, as a bittern emerges from the reeds. Both are acts of belonging, and both remind us that identity is not forged in loud declarations, but in the quiet repetition of what we love.

Bird watching teaches us to live with dual awareness of both the self and the world beyond the self. It shows us that looking closely is to care deeply and that noticing is to take part.

Whether we keep lists or walk with open eyes, whether we watch the birds with our family or in solitude, whether we belong to clubs or only to a window view and a garden feeder, we are part of a dispersed, gentle, and global community. A flock of one's own, and yet not ours alone.

I find there's a quiet comfort in this. That even when we watch birds alone, we are never truly isolated. Somewhere, someone else is also pausing to look up as they are listening for the same soft rustle or call across the field.

An identity does not have to be loud to be genuine, and a community does not have to be crowded to be authentic. Bird watching offers both subtle and enduring ways. It asks only that we pay attention, and in that attention, it gives us a sense of place, of belonging and continuity.

You may start watching birds and find, years later, that they have been watching you back. They have shaped how you move through the world, and they have introduced you, quietly, surely, to yourself and others.

And so we return, again and again, to the field, the window or the sky.

We are watching together.

Time, Patience, and Observation

We live in an age that resents waiting. Everything must be immediate, available, and streamable. Bird watching rebels against this, and through this rebellion, it teaches a different tempo: slow attention, long silence, and the subtle rewards of presence. To watch birds is to surrender to their schedule, not ours. In doing so, we are challenged to confront something elemental: the human relationship with time.

The Philosophy of Waiting: Time as Teacher

Philosophers have long pondered time as the great equaliser, the great revealer. For Heraclitus, time was a flow, a river we can never step into twice. For the Stoics, it was a gift that demanded our attention and reverence. Marcus Aurelius, in his *Meditations*, often reminded himself that everything passes, and thus everything must be accepted with grace. Bird watching makes these abstract lessons tangible. One sits, waits, breathes, and assumes that nature is not at one's disposal.

In Buddhism, the concept of mindfulness is inextricably linked with patience. One learns to dwell fully in each moment without clinging or resisting. The sound of a bird's call, the flick of a wing in the distance, the shadow cast by a passing hawk: where these are not merely objects of attention, but instead become the moment itself, the watcher and the watched collapse into one shared presence.

To wait for a bird that may never come is not foolishness; it is devotion. It is the kind of devotion that teaches us something about our inner states: our restlessness, our expectations, and our ability to be with what is. It is no accident that many spiritual traditions use nature as a metaphor for enlightenment. The bird appears when the mind is still.

Bird watching is, in many ways, a practical encounter with one of the oldest philosophical dilemmas: what is time? Is it simply a measure of movement? A ticking clock? Or is it something else, like a lived experience, an atmosphere, or a dimension of being?

Henri Bergson distinguished between *chronos*, the mechanical time of schedules and sequences, and *durée*, the lived duration of consciousness. The latter is what we encounter in the field. A moment of eye contact with a goldcrest can feel like a minute or an hour. The ticking stops. Time becomes *felt* rather than counted.

Martin Heidegger, in *Being and Time*, argued that our relationship to time determines our authenticity. We are thrown into a world already in motion, and yet we are called to own our existence by attending to its temporality. In other words, by facing time honestly. Bird watching offers this confrontation. It reminds us that we are not the masters of time, but its students.

In waiting, in silence, we reclaim a more original way of being by not controlling life but dwelling in it.

Simone Weil described attention as the highest form of generosity, even likening it to prayer. To attend to something without grasping, without wanting to own or use it, is to honour its essence. When we watch a bird without trying to photograph it, name it, or tick it off a list, we enter into a sacred state of attention. We watch it simply because it is *there*. This looks to purify our perception. It reorients us from consumption to contemplation.

There is also the ancient Greek distinction between *chronos* and *kairos*. *Chronos* is clock time, the quantitative, relentless, and indifferent. *Kairos*, by contrast, is qualitative time, the opportune moment, the right time, the time pregnant with meaning. A kestrel hovering at dusk, a heron lifting from the reeds at sunrise, are *kairotic* moments that are revealed. To be a bird watcher is to cultivate readiness for *kairos*.

This philosophy of waiting, of attentive stillness, runs counter to modernity. It is not only slower; it is deeper. It asks us not to escape time, but to re-enter it through a different door. And through that door, we might find not just birds, but ourselves.

Patience in a Culture of Speed

In contrast, our digital age is characterised by instant gratification, where everything from food delivery to information retrieval is designed to meet this expectation. Algorithms anticipate our desires before we articulate them. But bird watching refuses to be scheduled or predicted. The kingfisher will not ping your phone. The nightingale will not send a calendar invite. Their very existence is a rebuke to our need for control.

Slowness is not in vogue, and waiting is a nuisance. But what if the ability to wait is precisely what makes us human? In resisting the urge to act, to speak, to demand, we cultivate space for perception, for reflection, for care. Patience is a radical act.

The psychologist Viktor Frankl, in *Man's Search for Meaning*, emphasised the space between stimulus and response. It is in this space that our freedom lies. Bird watching enlarges that space.

You hear a rustle in the bush, do you rush over, or do you wait? You see a flash of feathers; do you grab your phone or observe? With each patient interaction, we resist the cultural script that tells us to consume, capture, and catalogue.

Psychological Virtues: Resilience, Presence, and the Long View

Bird watching sharpens the mind by softening it. We become more aware, less reactive. The discipline required to sit in silence for hours builds mental endurance. The unpredictability of sightings teaches us to be flexible. We do not control the outcome; we prepare the conditions.

Psychological studies on delayed gratification, such as Walter Mischel's marshmallow test, suggest that the ability to wait for a larger reward is correlated with higher levels of emotional intelligence, goal persistence, and even academic success. But beyond such measurable benefits, there is something more existential at play: the cultivation of presence.

Presence is not merely being in a place. It is being *with* the place.

Bird watching demands an attunement to the environment; its sounds, shifts in light, and subtle cues. It trains a kind of embodied intelligence. You begin to *feel* when something is about to happen as the forest quiets. The finches scatter. And then, perhaps, the owl arrives.

This heightened sensitivity is not just for sound for birding. It seeps into daily life. You become more aware of tone in conversation, more sensitive to mood, more attuned to what is left unsaid. Patience creates space, and in that space, perception deepens.

Research on *attention restoration theory* by Rachel and Stephen Kaplan suggests that natural environments help replenish our capacity for directed attention. Unlike urban environments, which demand constant mental effort to filter noise and stimulation, nature offers a form of *"soft fascination"* that engages the mind without exhausting it. Watching birds, especially in quiet or green environments, provides precisely this kind of restorative engagement.

The psychologist Mihaly Csikszentmihalyi, known for his work on *"flow states,"* described the optimal experience as one of complete immersion in a task that balances skill with challenge. Bird watching often invites this state. You lose track of time, fully engaged in observation, anticipation, and response. There is effort, but also absorption. You are no longer separate from the moment because you are in it.

Moreover, bird watching offers a form of cognitive therapy through the rhythm and repetition of its activities. The daily or weekly practice of watching builds a sense of coherence and control. This kind of routine is beneficial for individuals struggling with anxiety, burnout, or trauma. Some ecotherapy models now incorporate birding as a specific intervention, particularly for veterans with PTSD or individuals recovering from depressive episodes. The calming, non-demanding presence of birds, coupled with a sense of discovery, helps people reconnect with themselves and their surroundings.

Dopamine, often associated with reward and pleasure, is not just released when we receive something we desire but also during the anticipation of it. This is crucial in bird watching. The long wait, the patient scan, and the sudden glimpse trigger a sustained release of dopamine, not a high, but a hum of engagement. This slow, steady reward system contrasts with the spikes of social media or video games, which often lead to overstimulation and eventual burnout.

The patience cultivated in birding may serve as an antidote to a kind of cultural fatigue, helping to rewire our attention spans, retrain our expectations, and replenish our mental endurance. Bird watching becomes a practice of psychological resilience through its gift of renewal.

Personal Anecdotes: On the Edge of Seeing

A Danish birder once told me about her long search for a golden oriole. She had spent years hoping to spot one in her region, only to arrive too early or too late in the season. One spring, while recovering from surgery, she set up a chair by her back window and watched the trees. It was there, amid the green hush of a slow morning, that she finally saw it: a brilliant flash of yellow, moving like music through the poplar leaves. She didn't photograph it. She said the memory felt too complete to require evidence.

A young man from Nairobi spoke about his passion for the sunbird, a common species in Kenya, but one that holds special meaning for him. During his mother's illness, he would take short breaks from the hospital to walk near a local botanical garden. There, he often spotted a variable sunbird with iridescent plumage, darting among the flowers. He said the bird became a symbol of resilience, fragile, vivid, and present. After his mother passed away, he returned to that spot regularly. He never found the same sunbird, but others came to visit. He described those visits as a form of silent prayer.

In Cornwall, an elderly couple shared their decades-long ritual of watching the same peregrine pair that nested on the cliffs each spring. They kept journals, noting hatching dates and flight patterns, sharing the data with local conservation groups. When one of the falcons failed to return for one year, they mourned. But they returned anyway and were astonished when a new partner joined the surviving falcon the following spring. *"It's not just about the birds,"* the man said. *"It's about what the birds show us: grief, recovery, and partnership, the will to begin again."*

A teenager from Leipzig recounted how birdwatching helped him through the pandemic's isolation. Struggling with anxiety and distance from his friends, he began to keep a notebook of all the species he could identify from his apartment balcony. He described the moment he first saw a falcon flying high above the rooftops as an electric thrill, offering proof that wildness still existed, even above grey concrete. It was fleeting, but it shifted something in him. He began speaking more openly about his feelings with his parents. The bird, he said, had opened a window inside him.

These stories of longing, recovery, ritual, and revelation remind us that bird watching is a shared language. We may be scattered across the world, with different landscapes and species, but the act of watching connects us. Each bird, seen or missed, is a thread in a web of patient attention. These aren't tales of conquest. They are testaments to the quiet dignity of waiting. They are reminders that bird watching is an ongoing dialogue between presence and patience, hope and humility. It is a practice of being open, of allowing wonder to find you.

Garden Rituals: The Sacred Ordinary

You don't need to travel far to practise patience. The garden, the window ledge, or the small park near your home are temples of observation. I began a simple practice during lockdown: each morning, I would sit with a cup of tea by the window and watch who came to the balcony. At first, it was just tits and the odd blackbird that willingly flew high. But as weeks passed, a cast of characters emerged. There was a pigeon with a limp, a pair of jays that nested nearby and a magpie that never found the courage to enter the birdhouse.

By watching regularly, patterns emerged. The blackbird always sang at 5:30 a.m. The woodpecker came only when it rained. The robin grew brave enough to approach within a foot. These were not spectacular sightings. But they were intimate. Repetition became a relationship.

Rituals form. I found myself rising earlier, not out of obligation, but out of anticipation. I learned to greet the day with attention, to begin not with news or noise, but with stillness. The garden became a clock, a calendar, and a sanctuary. In a world obsessed with novelty, I found peace in the familiar.

Over time, the act of feeding birds became its quiet conversation. My wife adjusted the types of seed and added a shallow water dish. In the garden, the small log pile attracted insects, which in turn attracted robins and wrens. Even the local sparrowhawk began to make occasional passes, the top of the food chain woven into the morning scene. Every addition, every change, required observation. It was not a matter of imposing control, but of listening and responding.

There is something deeply restorative about this process. The garden becomes more than a plot of land; instead, it becomes a space of ritual, a theatre of patience, a mirror of one's internal seasons. Some mornings are vibrant with activity. Others are still and grey. And yet both hold value.

I remember one morning in midwinter. Frost coated the grass. I doubted anything would come. But just as the sun edged over the treetops, a blackcap landed on the frozen apple I had left out. Its feathers fluffed against the cold, and it stayed for nearly ten minutes, pecking and pausing. I didn't move. I barely breathed. In that moment, I felt more present, more awake, than I had in days.

Such moments are not rare if you practise the art of noticing. Patience becomes more than a waiting game as it becomes a way of seeing, a form of devotion, and a posture of readiness.

The Watcher Changes

Perhaps the most profound truth of all is that over time, it is not the birds that change, but the watcher. What begins as an interest, or even a pastime, often grows into something far more meaningful. We start with a desire to see. We end with a willingness to witness.

One birder described this change as a kind of internal softening. He no longer rushed toward every call or chased after rarities. Instead, he began to notice the quiet things: the way a chiffchaff flutters between reeds, the slow circling of a buzzard on a cloudy day. What he once might have dismissed as uneventful now became meaningful. This transformation, from the expectation of spectacle to the appreciation of nuance, is perhaps the deepest gift of the practice.

To become a bird watcher is to accept that we are always watching through the lens of change. Seasons shift, habitats evolve and even our own bodies age. The birds we once found common may become scarce; others may arrive unexpectedly. The passage of time becomes visible not just in plumage and migration but in ourselves in the way we stand, wait, and feel.

One woman, who had been birding for over forty years, spoke of the sorrow she felt when the nightjars no longer returned to her favourite heath. She mourned their silence, their absence, like an old friend no longer answering the phone. But she also spoke of a new joy: hearing a treecreeper for the first time in a local woodland she had never visited before. *"It's not the same,"* she said, *"but it's still a kind of grace."*

Bird watching teaches us to make peace with absence. It asks us to remain present even when what we hoped for does not appear. And this, too, is a life lesson, and that is to show up with attention, even when there's nothing to gain. To witness what is, not just what we desire.

As time passes, we become more porous. The watching becomes less about the bird and more about the act itself, the posture of stillness, the rhythm of breathing and the quiet ritual of arrival and departure. We begin to watch ourselves watching. And in doing so, we see how we've changed.

Patience is no longer a strategy. It becomes a temperamental way of inhabiting time.

Closing Reflection

To observe birds is to step outside ourselves. It is to practice humility in the face of time and to honour life on its terms. In a world of rush and noise, bird watching whispers: slow down. Be still. Wait. And in that waiting, find yourself returned to the rhythm of the world.

Bird watching is not a sport. It is not a quest. It is a form of remembering, remembering how to look, how to listen, and how to be. The bird will come. Or it won't. Either way, you have seen something rare: the unfolding of time, not as an enemy, but as a teacher.

When we learn to wait, to attend, to be, we are no longer just observers of birds. We become participants in the greater ecology of presence. We re-enter a world not made for speed or noise, but for cycles, stillness, and song.

And so we wait, and watch, and are changed.

Technology in Bird Watching

What happens when one of the most ancient, patient, and grounded human activities meets the tools of the digital age? Bird watching, once marked by silence and slow observation, is increasingly shaped by optics, algorithms, and networks. The field guide has evolved into an app: a sketchpad, a high-resolution lens, a morning walk, and a shared stream of data.

For many, this evolution is exciting. Technology has opened doors, allowing us to identify birdsong using artificial intelligence, track migration routes via satellite, and share sightings across continents in real time. Birders are no longer isolated observers but members of a connected global community.

And yet, there is unease. Has something been lost in the shift? Has the screen dimmed the sky? Does technology enhance our bond with birds, or does it subtly replace it with a bond to our own devices?

This chapter explores that tension as a meditation rather than being polemic. We will walk through the history of birding technology, consider its benefits and risks, reflect on philosophical and ethical concerns, and hear stories from those who have found both delight and distraction in its tools. Ultimately, we ask: how can we embrace innovation without losing the soul of the practice?

A Brief History of Birding Technology

To understand how modern technology fits into bird watching, it helps to look back at how the tools of the trade have evolved. In the early days of ornithology and recreational bird observation, dating back to the 18th and 19th centuries, birding was primarily a pursuit of scholars, naturalists, and hunters. The earliest bird watchers relied on field notes, telescopes, and artistic sketches to document their observations. The process was painstakingly slow, and identification often required encyclopaedic memory and comparative anatomy.

Field guides changed everything. The publication of Roger Tory Peterson's *A Field Guide to the Birds* in 1934 marked a turning point. Suddenly, birds could be identified in the field by amateurs using visual clues rather than specimen collection. This was, in its way, a technological leap: the portable book as an optical and cognitive tool.

Binoculars quickly followed as the next great equaliser. World War I and World War II had seen a boom in optical innovation, and surplus military binoculars became widely available. These affordable tools gave everyday people the chance to see birds, even from a distance, without disturbing them. The optics may have been heavy and imperfect, but they allowed birding to spread beyond the lab, the elite drawing rooms, or the hunting lodge.

By the 1970s and '80s, many birders were recording bird calls with cassette tapes, cataloguing species on paper checklists, and carrying field scopes weighing several kilograms. Slide film photography became a means of documenting rare sightings, although the equipment remained prohibitively expensive for most.

The digital revolution of the late 1990s and early 2000s opened an entirely new chapter. Digital cameras became more affordable, more portable, and increasingly powerful. At the same time, the internet allowed for the creation of global databases, listservs, and birding forums. The combination of digital photography and online sharing created what some called the *"birding renaissance"*. It was now possible to photograph a bird, post it within minutes, and receive feedback from experienced birders halfway across the globe.

Smartphones then became the ultimate multipurpose tool. Not only could you photograph and record audio, but you could carry entire libraries of birdsong, checklists, maps, and migration charts in your pocket. With apps like BirdNET and Merlin, even those with little experience could identify species using machine learning. Suddenly, a prospect that once seemed like science fiction has become the standard.

Today, birders walk into the field equipped with lightweight optics, AI-powered apps, and GPS-enabled digital notebooks. Some carry drones. Others wear sound-recording backpacks or deploy motion-triggered cameras near nests. Bird watching has become high-tech. And yet, the essential act, that of the human being standing still, eyes raised, and waiting, remains unchanged.

Optics: The Gateway Technology

The oldest companion in modern bird watching remains the binocular. A simple pair of optics transforms distant movement into a recognisable form of colour, posture, and the flicker of a wing. Binoculars have long been celebrated not as distractions but as extensions of the eye, honouring the natural encounter while enhancing its detail. They allow us to witness birds without intrusion, enabling us to remain respectful observers from a distance.

Over time, optical technologies have become more refined. The difference between budget and high-end binoculars or spotting scopes can be dramatic, particularly in terms of image clarity, brightness, edge sharpness, and low-light visibility. Yet, despite the technical improvements, the fundamental relationship remains the same as that of a human to a bird, with vision guiding flight. There is still something analogue, still intimate about the act of lifting binoculars and scanning the trees.

For many, the first experience of seeing the iridescent flash of a kingfisher or the intricate pattern of a wader's feathers through good binoculars or a telescope is unforgettable. It is technology in the service of awe.

Cameras and the Age of Capture

Then came the camera. What began as field sketching through painstaking drawings in notebooks has evolved into a domain of photography, ranging from DSLRs to mirrorless systems and now even smartphones mounted on digiscoping adapters. Birding and photography have become twin hobbies, often inseparable.

Photography allows for documentation, study, and sharing. It captures moments that might otherwise be lost to memory. For many, it deepens their appreciation of studying the curve of a beak or identifying plumage variations visible only in still images. Photos make the invisible visible.

But there is a tension. In the pursuit of the perfect shot, something may be lost in the silent communion with the moment unmediated. The presence becomes performance for the camera and ultimately for the online gallery. Some birders speak of missing the bird itself while fumbling with settings. The technology, meant to preserve the moment, can sometimes displace it.

And yet, others argue that photography creates a more enduring love. Reviewing images, revisiting memories, and even printing photos can extend the emotional lifespan of a single sighting. A bird seen once becomes a bird remembered many times.

Apps, Databases, and the Shared Field

In recent years, digital tools have revolutionised birding. Apps like Merlin, eBird, iNaturalist, BirdNET, and Xeno-Canto have opened up new dimensions of identification, tracking, and community.

Merlin offers field guide tools and AI-assisted identification, where we upload a photo, and it guesses the species. BirdNET recognises birdsong from audio recordings. Xeno-Canto is a crowdsourced repository of bird calls from around the world. eBird allows users to log their sightings, contributing to one of the most significant citizen science projects on the planet.

For beginners, these tools offer reassurance and empowerment. You don't need to memorise every warbler call because you can confirm, replay, and compare. For seasoned birders, they provide data, migration insights, and a sense of contribution. You are no longer watching alone. You are watching as part of a global network.

But here, too, questions arise. Does constant consulting break the rhythm of being present? Does reliance on algorithms atrophy our memory and skills? Are we observing birds or interacting with screens? The paradox of the birding app is that it makes identification easier, but observation harder when the eyes turn downward to look at the phone.

Live Streams, Nest Cams, and Virtual Watching

The digital era has also brought birds into our homes. Live feeds from nest cams allow us to watch peregrines on city towers or ospreys feeding their young. Nature is now streamable.

For many, this is a miracle. It educates, inspires, and provides access to those who are typically underrepresented in the field, including children, the elderly, and individuals with disabilities. As a result, it draws public attention to conservation, species survival, and ecological integrity.

Yet virtual watching is not the same as wild watching. There is no wind in your face and no bird sound echoing through the trees. The moment is observed, but it is not shared. It is informational, and not relational.

Still, there is beauty in this reach with technology as an invitation rather than a replacement for watching, when the screen can awaken the desire to step outside.

Does Technology Enhance or Detract?

The question of technology's role in bird watching is not binary. It is a matter of balance, of awareness. Like any tool, technology reflects the intention behind its use. A camera can become a weapon of intrusion or a brush of reverence just as much as an app can be a crutch or a tutor.

Some birders insist on *"bare birding"*—no camera, no phone, no gear, only binoculars. Others embrace the full suite of tools, from parabolic microphones to motion-triggered cameras. Most fall somewhere in between.

Technology can deepen knowledge, connect people, democratise access, and aid conservation. But it can also distract, distort, and commercialise the experience. The key question becomes: are we using these tools to see the bird more clearly, or to see ourselves reflected in some way?

Philosophy and the Wild Interface

The intersection of technology and bird watching invites not only practical but also philosophical inquiry. At stake is not merely what we see, but *how* we see and whether the very act of watching changes when it is filtered through devices.

Albert Borgmann, in his exploration of the "device paradigm," argued that modern technology tends to conceal the richness of traditional practices. In birding, this might mean that using an app to identify a bird in seconds could shortcut the deeper process of learning through repeated listening to calls, puzzling over plumage and posture, and accepting uncertainty. When technology delivers answers without requiring engagement, it risks severing us from the patience and humility that bird watching teaches.

Heidegger went further, warning against the reduction of nature to a mere "standing-reserve", creating a stockpile of data points to be accessed, stored, and used. A bird is no longer a creature in its own right, but a record on eBird, a target for a checklist, and a high-resolution photo to share. The wild becomes a means to an end, and we, despite our reverence, risk becoming managers rather than witnesses.

Contrast this with the ethos of Henry David Thoreau, who saw in nature not a problem to be solved but a mystery to be dwelt within. Thoreau's long walks with his notebooks and his attentive gaze represent a kind of analogue mindfulness that stands in quiet defiance of digital immediacy. Would Thoreau use Merlin or eBird? Perhaps. But only, one imagines, after a long time spent listening in silence, with no need for confirmation.

And yet, not all philosophies warn against technology. Bruno Latour, among others, suggests that humans and tools are co-constitutive, that is, we understand the world through the very means by which we interact with it. A bird song app, then, is not necessarily an obstacle to presence. It can be a prosthetic for deeper perception. A microphone doesn't remove us from nature, and it may extend our hearing into ranges we could never access on our own.

Rachel Carson, too, though writing long before apps and smartphones, believed in the role of science and education in fostering awe. She argued that wonder and knowledge were not opposites but companions. Her writings invite us to consider whether the proper use of technology could help more people *see*, not just look, provided we don't confuse the screen for the scene.

Ultimately, the philosophical question is not about whether we use technology, but whether we use it *well*. Do our tools deepen our reverence, or do they distract from it? Do they amplify our sense of participation, or do they flatten it into consumption?

Perhaps the answer lies in intention. If we approach the bird as a gift, rather than a trophy, or as a moment to be experienced rather than a record to be broken, then our use of technology can remain in harmony with the ethics of presence. A tool in the hand does not preclude stillness in the heart.

Ethical Concerns and Conservation Tensions

Alongside the philosophical debate lies an increasingly urgent ethical conversation. Despite its numerous benefits, technology can have unintended consequences for birds and their habitats. In the hands of the unaware or the overly eager, it can cross lines.

Playback apps, for instance, allow birders to play recordings of bird calls to attract hidden individuals. While this can help with elusive species, overuse, especially during the breeding season, can cause stress, territorial confusion, and even nest abandonment. A single misplaced call may not matter, but repeated disturbances in popular birding areas can have a cumulative impact.

Drones provide stunning aerial footage and offer access to previously inaccessible terrain. But when flown too close to nesting sites, they can cause alarm or provoke defensive behaviours. Birds of prey, in particular, are sensitive to intrusion, and some have been known to abandon nests due to repeated drone activity.

Camera flashes, extended presence in fragile habitats, or even geotagging photos of endangered species can inadvertently endanger birds by attracting crowds or predators. Some birders now deliberately obscure the locations of rare sightings to protect vulnerable populations.

There are also concerns about the data collected by citizen science platforms, which gather enormous amounts of information, including precise coordinates of bird sightings. While this data is valuable for research and conservation, it can be misused. Egg collectors, unethical photographers, or wildlife traders have been known to exploit such platforms.

To address these challenges, many birding organisations and forums have developed ethical guidelines. The American Birding Association's Code of Birding Ethics, for instance, urges restraint in playback use, respect for private property, and prioritising bird welfare over photographs. Apps like eBird now allow users to mark sightings as "sensitive," limiting their public visibility.

Technology, then, is not inherently harmful. But it demands *ethics in practice*. Awareness, restraint, and community standards become crucial. A drone can be used for habitat surveys that help protect nesting sites. A microphone can be used to record calls for monitoring endangered species, and a camera can document the illegal destruction of wetlands.

The line between helpful and harmful lies not in the tool, but in the attitude. If we approach birds with reverence rather than conquest, then even the most advanced technologies can be used in the service of wonder, not disruption.

The philosopher Albert Borgmann warned of the *"device paradigm,"* in which technology delivers commodities without context. In traditional practices, the means were as necessary as the end. In bird watching, this means that finding a bird through listening, intuition, and presence is not the same as being told by a GPS ping.

Heidegger, too, feared the enframing of nature as a resource of something to be calculated, predicted, and harnessed. When we map migration to the minute or photograph every moment, are we honouring the bird, or converting it into data?

Yet others, such as Bruno Latour, argue that technology is part of our ecology and that it does not separate us from nature, but instead redefines how we engage with the world; the microphone, the scope, and the app have all become prosthetics of perception. The question is not whether technology belongs in bird watching, but what kind of relationship we want with it. Are we seeking a deeper presence, efficient acquisition of wonder, or mastery?

In the end, the bird remains outside us, that is, wild, independent, and inscrutable. Technology may bring us closer to its image, its pattern, its call. But only our stillness, our willingness to be changed by the encounter, brings us closer to the bird itself.

Social Media and the Self in Birding

One of the quieter revolutions in bird watching has taken place not in the field, but online. Social media platforms, especially Instagram, YouTube, Twitter (now X), and TikTok, have created a new layer of engagement between birders and the birds they watch. Sightings can now be shared within seconds, often accompanied by vivid images, filters, captions, hashtags, and emotional narratives. For better or worse, birding has entered the age of the curated self.

There are clear benefits to this transformation. Social media has made birding more visible, accessible, and culturally relevant. Young people discover it through reels of urban falcons or quirky videos of woodpeckers. Communities form around shared interests, photography styles, or local hotspots. Hashtags like #birdwatching, #backyardbirds, or #birdnerd have become miniature meeting places. Education, identification, and connection thrive in these digital spaces.

But the shift also carries subtle risks. Bird watching, long a refuge from performance and competition, is now in contact with the world of likes, followers, and engagement metrics. The temptation arises to photograph the rarest bird, the best pose, the most dramatic moment, not always for oneself, but for an audience. The gaze shifts, ever so slightly, from the bird to the mirror.

Some birders report a sense of disconnection when sharing becomes habitual. The quiet satisfaction of a morning in the woods is sometimes undercut by the urge to edit and post, to document rather than dwell. Others describe a growing anxiety around being *"first"* to report a sighting or capturing something *"share-worthy."*

On the other hand, many find that documenting and sharing deepens their commitment to the craft. Editing a photo can be a form of reverence. Writing about a sighting may become an act of storytelling, of remembering. When done with care, these digital artefacts become modern field notes, like snapshots of time, place, and perspective.

It is not the medium itself that poses the challenge, but the mindset it encourages. When used with intention and balance, social media can amplify the joy of discovery and help bridge communities across continents. When used unreflectively, it can turn even the most personal encounter into content.

A thoughtful birder once put it this way: *"If I photograph a bird, it's because I want to honour it. But if I only go out looking for a photo, I've already missed the bird."*

Bird watching on social media is neither a saviour nor a corrupter of the craft. It is simply another lens, one that magnifies both beauty and ego. The challenge, as ever, is to look through it without losing sight of the bird.

Global and Intergenerational Stories from the Digital Field

One birder told me about using a parabolic microphone to detect night migrants. Alone on his rooftop, he recorded hundreds of nocturnal flight calls of species he never would have identified by sight. He described the experience as ghostly and magical, likening it to an unseen river of sound flowing overhead. Technology had opened a new dimension of birding, one invisible to the naked eye.

Another birder, newly retired, discovered the joy of digiscoping with her phone. With shaky hands, she'd found traditional photography hard. But using her scope and a simple adapter, she began capturing astonishing images of marsh harriers and snipe. She printed them into a book for her grandchildren. *"It gave me a reason to go out,"* she said. *"And a way to come home with something to show."*

Of course, not all tales are triumphs. One enthusiastic beginner, keen to record a rare wood warbler, ended up playing the call on a speaker, accidentally creating confusion in a breeding territory. Another dropped his phone into a reedbed while trying to photograph a bittern. *"The bird stayed dry. I didn't."*

Technology expands the spectrum of experience: from the sublime to the silly. But always, it places us in a dialogue with birds, with each other, with ourselves.

In a small village in India, a retired schoolteacher uses a basic Android phone and the eBird app to contribute weekly sightings from his rooftop. He doesn't speak English fluently, but with the app's interface in his regional language and help from his grandson, he's logged over 200 species. His data is now part of a global conservation effort.

In New York City, a teenage birder documents peregrine falcons nesting on a high-rise office building. Her short-form videos, which are equal parts artful, humorous, and educational, have gone viral. In one, she narrates a chase sequence with music; in another, she explains peregrine courtship while sketching on her tablet. Her digital savvy has attracted urban youth to birding in a way few conservation campaigns have.

In a small community in rural Kenya, a conservation NGO trained local teenagers to use GPS-tagged cameras and acoustic sensors to monitor the habitat of the endangered Sharpe's longclaw. They now lead tours, educate tourists, and upload data to international networks, transforming passive observation into a source of employment and stewardship.

Not all generational divides are digital. An elderly couple in Sweden, devoted analogue birders for decades, once scoffed at apps until their granddaughter helped them identify a Eurasian pygmy owl using BirdNET. *"We still trust our ears more than machines,"* the woman said, *"but now the machine helps confirm what we already feel."*

These stories echo across cultures and generations. Technology does not replace the heart of birding. Instead, it reveals new ways for people to fall in love with it. Whether through a phone screen or a worn field guide, the moment of wonder remains the same, regardless if it is a flicker of wings or a bright call in the leaves, and yet, there is the stillness that follows. But always, it places us in a dialogue with birds, with each other, with ourselves.

The Future of Birding Technology

As technology continues to evolve rapidly, the future of bird watching may look very different, yet strangely familiar. The core activity will always be the same: attention, presence, and delight. But the tools we use to get there may become more integrated, immersive, and intelligent.

Imagine lightweight augmented reality (AR) glasses that project species information directly into your field of vision, eliminating the need for a phone or guidebook. A warbler lands on a branch, and subtle data of plumage ID tips, migratory patterns, and recent sightings appear in the corner of your lens. This kind of wearable technology is already being prototyped for industrial and educational purposes, where its arrival in birding may not be far off.

Artificial intelligence will likely play an increasingly significant role in real-time identification, not only for visual sightings but also for complex soundscapes. Machine learning systems are becoming adept at distinguishing multiple overlapping bird calls, tracking specific individuals, and mapping migratory trends using live audio. BirdNET and similar tools may evolve into continuous, unobtrusive environmental monitors of systems that learn from your environment while teaching you about it.

Citizen science will also expand. Future birding apps might include collaborative swarm features, where real-time data from multiple users creates dynamic bird distribution maps that adjust by the hour. This could revolutionise not only recreational birding but also conservation and emergency habitat protection.

On the conservation side, bio-logging and satellite telemetry will become more refined. Miniaturised trackers may allow safe monitoring of even small songbirds, providing detailed insights into global flyways, stopover threats, and long-term climate impacts. With the help of quantum sensors and high-altitude drones, scientists may gain a more granular picture of avian life than ever before.

Yet as these tools become increasingly powerful, the philosophical and ethical questions they raise will grow as well. If a headset can instantly identify every bird for you, will the watcher still develop the skill, the patience, the intimacy? Will field craft fade into dependency? Or will it evolve into a new form, and that is of one that marries instinct and interface, memory and machine?

Some envision a backlash of a return to analogue birding as a kind of meditative retreat. Already, movements like *"slow birding"* and *"deep ecology"* advocate for low-tech or no-tech experiences, focusing on presence over productivity. These parallel futures, digital and distributed, versus grounded and slow, may not be mutually exclusive. Instead, they may shape a new hybrid culture: one that embraces tools when they serve insight, but knows when to set them down.

As birders, we will likely live in both worlds. Some mornings will be logged, shared, and tagged. Others will be quiet, undocumented, and forgotten, yet felt. The future of birding technology lies not in its gadgets, but in its wisdom, the wisdom to choose how, when, and why we watch.

Conservation Tech in Action

Beyond recreational use, technology is quietly transforming conservation work. Tools once confined to research labs or military use are now being deployed to protect endangered species and habitats, and birders are playing an increasingly important role in this effort.

One of the most significant breakthroughs has been in satellite telemetry. Tiny GPS tags, attached to migratory birds such as the spoon-billed sandpiper and the bar-tailed godwit, have enabled scientists to track entire migratory journeys with astonishing detail. These insights have revealed previously unknown stopover sites in wetlands and feeding grounds critical to survival, and have led to targeted protection efforts, including the creation of temporary sanctuaries during peak migration.

In the Amazon rainforest, remote acoustic monitoring systems have been used to detect the calls of endangered antbirds and manakins in regions too dense or dangerous to explore regularly on foot. These solar-powered units continuously record data, which is then fed into AI systems that flag species of interest. Conservationists now use this information to map biodiversity hotspots and areas of illegal logging, often in near real-time.

In urban areas, technology has also enabled citizen-led protection efforts. In London, thermal cameras and rooftop monitors have been used to track the success of peregrine falcon nests. In Cape Town, real-time alerts from tagged African penguins help rangers reduce human disturbance and guide tourists to respectful viewing locations.

Apps like eBird and iNaturalist serve not just as logbooks but as platforms for ecological vigilance. A sudden drop in sightings in one region can alert researchers to pollution events, land clearance, or the emergence of new diseases. In Australia, user-submitted data helped map the spread of avian flu; in the U.S., it has been used to track the fallout of wildfire smoke on migratory patterns.

Crucially, these efforts highlight a shift in birding from passive observation to active guardianship. Whether by uploading a photo, flagging a disturbance, or donating data to a conservation project, the modern birder now participates in a wider ecological intelligence. Technology, in this sense, is not just a lens; it is a multifaceted tool. It is a bridge.

Toward a Thoughtful Birding Future

There is no going back to a purely analogue world. And perhaps we wouldn't want to. The tools of modern birding, when used with care, can enhance our capacity for awe, expand our reach across space, and deepen our sense of connection.

But let us not forget the essence of a child watching a robin for the first time. A seasoned birder returning to the same marsh every year. The hush before dawn. The sudden arrival.

Technology can help us see better, but only attention allows us to watch honestly.

In bird watching, as in life, the tool is never the goal. The goal is presence. And for that, no device will ever surpass the stillness of the human eye and the openness of the waiting heart.

Cultural Perspectives and Symbolism

Birds have long captured humanity's imagination, transcending mere fascination to embody profound symbolic meanings across diverse cultures. From mythology to folklore, from literature to philosophy, birds serve as rich metaphors that reflect humanity's values, fears, hopes, and spiritual beliefs. Birds, with their ability to fly and traverse between earth and sky, often symbolise freedom, transcendence, and connection to the divine or spiritual realms, capturing universal aspirations and existential curiosities.

Throughout history, societies have projected their deepest beliefs and values onto birds, viewing them as messengers, omens, protectors, or guides, bridging the natural and supernatural worlds. Exploring these symbolic narratives provides valuable insights into how societies globally construct their relationships with nature, define their collective identities, and express their cultural distinctiveness.

By examining the diverse symbolic roles birds occupy across cultures, we gain a deeper appreciation for the intricate ways in which human societies interpret the natural world, navigate existential questions, and forge connections that sustain cultural continuity and ecological harmony.

Birds in Mythology, Folklore, and Global Symbolism

Throughout history, birds have prominently featured in mythologies and folktales, becoming vessels for spiritual meanings, moral lessons, and divine messages.

In ancient Egypt, birds such as the ibis and falcon were deeply symbolic. Horus, depicted as a falcon, represented kingship, protection, and the sun's regenerative power. Ancient Egyptian texts describe Horus's battle against his uncle Set, symbolising the struggle between order and chaos. The falcon thus became a critical symbol of the pharaoh's authority, reinforcing the concept of divine kingship. Similarly, Thoth, portrayed with an ibis head, was the god of wisdom, writing, and judgment. Detailed accounts of Thoth's role in the weighing of souls depict his pivotal position as a mediator between the gods and humans, reinforcing the symbolic power of birds in Egyptian religious life.

Greek mythology richly integrates birds as symbols of wisdom, prophecy, and fate. Athena, the goddess of wisdom, is often accompanied by an owl, symbolising wisdom, vigilance, and insight. Mythological narratives usually depict the owl as a guide, offering profound wisdom during pivotal moments, particularly in Homeric tales and classical Greek dramas. Conversely, Apollo's raven symbolises prophecy and misfortune. In one myth, Apollo sent a white raven to spy on his lover, Coronis. When the raven reported her infidelity, Apollo turned its feathers black as punishment, symbolising the heavy consequences that knowledge can entail.

Norse mythology deeply incorporates ravens through Odin's companions, Huginn and Muninn, who symbolise thought and memory. Each day, these ravens journeyed across the nine worlds, returning to whisper their findings into Odin's ears. This daily ritual underscores profound Norse philosophical themes regarding the essential nature of knowledge, perception, and the interconnectedness of all realms of existence. Ravens thus embody the depth and complexity of Norse spiritual and existential thought.

In Native American spirituality, birds play a crucial symbolic role across diverse tribes and regions. The eagle, revered universally, symbolises courage, strength, and spiritual transcendence. Eagle feathers hold deep ceremonial significance and are used in rituals marking essential community decisions, personal milestones, and spiritual healing ceremonies. Tribes such as the Lakota and Cherokee narrate elaborate eagle legends emphasising bravery, resilience, and divine connection. Similarly, tribes like the Hopi and Pueblo have complex narratives surrounding birds, such as the crow and owl, which highlight the nuanced meanings of transformation, insight, and caution.

Mesoamerican cultures, particularly the Aztecs and Mayans, revered birds significantly. The feathered serpent god Quetzalcoatl represents creation, rebirth, and the cycles of life and death. Mythological accounts describe Quetzalcoatl descending from the heavens, symbolising the union of the earthly and divine realms, and underscoring the transformative power that birds embodied within these civilisations.

In Hindu mythology, Garuda, a divine eagle, symbolises immense strength, courage, and spiritual liberation. Serving as the mount of the god Vishnu, Garuda embodies courage and unwavering loyalty. Detailed stories depict Garuda's battles with serpents, symbolising the triumph of righteousness over evil forces, reinforcing moral teachings through vivid avian symbolism.

Aboriginal Australian traditions incorporate birds deeply into Dreamtime stories that detail the creation of the world. The emu, in particular, symbolises resourcefulness, endurance, and survival. Dreamtime narratives often depict the emu traversing challenging landscapes, embodying essential cultural virtues necessary for thriving in Australia's harsh environments.

Polynesian culture extensively incorporates birds into its navigational traditions and spiritual symbolism. Frigatebirds are especially significant, regarded as ancestral spirits guiding navigators safely across vast ocean expanses. Polynesian myths frequently recount voyages inspired and guided by observing bird patterns, underscoring their crucial role in Polynesian cultural identity and maritime expertise.

By deeply embedding bird symbolism within these extensive cultural mythologies, humanity reinforces essential values, moral lessons, and spiritual beliefs. Birds serve as profound symbolic vehicles, connecting human consciousness with the natural and spiritual worlds, and emphasising their crucial role in shaping global cultural identities.

Expanded Cultural Symbolism of Specific Birds

Owls: Owls carry a variety of symbolic meanings. Western cultures associate owls predominantly with wisdom, a tradition rooted in Greek mythology. Indigenous American tribes, however, view owls as symbols of transformation, caution, and death, and deeply respect their presence. Among these tribes, owl calls or sightings might indicate a time of significant change or act as a warning to be mindful.

In Japan, owls are widely regarded as symbols of luck, protection, and prosperity, frequently depicted in artworks, charms, and home decorations intended to attract good fortune. Pueblo and Hopi legends further highlight owl symbolism, describing owls as guardians and messengers that guide community decisions and individual spiritual journeys, emphasising the interconnectedness between humans and the natural world.

Ravens: Ravens feature prominently across global mythologies as both prophetic and trickster figures. In Celtic and Norse traditions, ravens symbolise wisdom, war, and prophecy, frequently associated with battlefield omens and spiritual messages. Norse tales often depict ravens guiding warriors and kings, symbolising strategic insight and divine guidance.

The indigenous peoples of the Pacific Northwest portray ravens as tricksters, embodying creativity, humour, and moral ambiguity, and playing essential roles in teaching stories about morality and life's paradoxes.

Edgar Allan Poe famously encapsulates raven symbolism in his poem "The Raven": *"Once upon a midnight dreary, while I pondered, weak and weary, Over many a quaint and curious volume of forgotten lore—While I nodded, nearly napping, suddenly there came a tapping, As if someone were gently rapping, rapping at my chamber door. "'Tis some visitor," I muttered, "tapping at my chamber door—Only this and nothing more.""*

The repeated refrain *"Nevermore"* embodies existential dread and profound loss, significantly impacting literary tradition and popular culture, symbolising despair, mourning, and the eternal nature of grief. This complete poem can be found at the front of the book.

Cranes: Cranes symbolise grace, fidelity, and longevity, particularly celebrated in East Asian cultures. Detailed narratives from Japanese and Chinese traditions often depict cranes as spiritual creatures that promise eternal happiness and prosperity. Japanese folklore usually portrays cranes as mystical beings capable of living for a thousand years, embodying immortality and fidelity, as illustrated in the poignant tale of the *"Crane Wife."*

Festivals, dances, and ceremonies dedicated to cranes exemplify their deep cultural integration and reverence. In European folklore, cranes symbolise vigilance and caution, underscoring cultural admiration for their alertness. Their migrations were historically viewed as markers of changing seasons, symbolising the cyclical nature of time.

By deeply embedding bird symbolism within these extensive cultural mythologies, humanity reinforces essential values, moral lessons, and spiritual beliefs. Birds serve as profound symbolic vehicles, connecting human consciousness with the natural and spiritual worlds, and emphasising their crucial role in shaping global cultural identities.

Philosophical Perspectives: Symbolism and Nature

Symbolism profoundly influences our philosophical and ethical relationships with the natural world. Philosophers such as Ernst Cassirer and Carl Jung discuss symbols as fundamental frameworks that shape human perceptions of reality. Cassirer emphasises that symbolic systems, including language, art, and myth, fundamentally structure human experience, providing meaningful ways to interpret the complexities of nature and existence. Carl Jung further explores symbolism as a means for accessing deeper layers of the human psyche, connecting collective unconscious archetypes with universal natural phenomena, often using bird symbolism to illustrate these profound connections.

Birds, laden with symbolic meanings, illustrate humanity's deep-rooted need to understand the natural world through metaphors. The flight of birds, their seasonal migrations, and unique behaviours frequently serve as potent symbols reflecting human aspirations, struggles, and transformations. Friedrich Nietzsche's reflections highlight how symbolism reveals human existential truths and internal conflicts. Nietzsche views symbolic interactions with nature as indicative of humanity's profound desires and fears, emphasising that symbols help reconcile human consciousness with the often indifferent or enigmatic natural world.

The symbolic values attributed to different birds reflect cultural priorities, affecting attitudes towards conservation and environmental stewardship. Positive symbols, such as cranes representing longevity and prosperity or eagles symbolising courage and strength, typically inspire protective and conservationist attitudes. These symbolic interpretations encourage communities to actively engage in preservation efforts, promoting respect and harmony with natural ecosystems.

Conversely, negative or ambiguous symbolism associated with birds like ravens or vultures may lead to misunderstanding, persecution, or neglect, underscoring the need for more balanced symbolic frameworks.

Philosophers such as Heidegger and Derrida further elaborate on the role of symbolism in shaping human ecological ethics. Heidegger's philosophy suggests that symbolic thinking shapes our fundamental relationship with *"being,"* encouraging humans to contemplate their interconnectedness with all forms of life.

Derrida's deconstructive approach challenges traditional symbolic hierarchies, advocating for a reconsideration and redefinition of human relationships with nature. Both philosophers emphasise the importance of critically reflecting upon existing symbolic meanings to promote more compassionate, sustainable, and inclusive ecological practices.

Expanding these philosophical discussions deepens our understanding of how symbolism influences ecological consciousness and ethical responsibility. By critically engaging with symbolic meanings and exploring new symbolic narratives, societies can cultivate a more holistic, empathetic, and sustainable relationship with nature, reflecting evolving ecological awareness and responsibility.

International Bird Watching: Cultural Reflections

Bird watching provides intimate insights into diverse cultural relationships with nature. Observing cranes at Kushiro Shitsugen National Park in Japan, bird watchers encounter firsthand the cultural reverence for these birds, understanding them as symbols of harmony, fidelity, and good fortune. Local traditions, narratives, and conservation efforts around cranes illustrate deeply embedded cultural values. Japanese crane festivals often incorporate dances and rituals that celebrate the bird's elegance and symbolic importance, offering bird watchers immersive experiences into the cultural traditions and their spiritual significance.

In India, birdwatchers observing vultures gain insight into the complex cultural symbolism associated with them. Historically revered in Hindu traditions as purifiers, vultures face contemporary ecological challenges. Traditional Hindu practices once relied heavily on vultures for the ritualistic disposal of bodies, symbolising purification and rebirth. Discussions with local conservationists reveal cultural efforts to reconcile traditional reverence with modern conservation needs, highlighting the vultures' symbolic and ecological importance. Initiatives such as the establishment of protected vulture habitats emphasise the community's efforts to sustain traditional cultural values while addressing modern environmental challenges.

Birding expeditions in Scotland's seabird colonies or Iceland's remote landscapes offer further cultural exploration. Scotland's coastal communities tell vivid stories of puffins and seabirds, deeply embedded in local folklore as symbols of seaside life, resilience, and maritime heritage. Icelandic folklore surrounding ravens reveals complex narratives of prophecy, wisdom, and caution, reflecting deep cultural connections to the natural landscape and spiritual beliefs. Local narratives shared during these expeditions significantly enrich the bird watchers 'understanding of regional identity, heritage, and environmental ethics.

Bird-watching experiences in tropical regions, such as Costa Rica, further deepen cultural reflections. Observations of brightly coloured toucans, parrots, and hummingbirds introduce bird watchers to the cultural symbolism of vibrant life, renewal, and spiritual vitality in indigenous narratives. Interactions with local guides, storytellers, and communities during these excursions offer meaningful insights into how tropical bird species shape cultural practices, storytelling traditions, and ecological awareness.

Extended personal narratives that describe interactions with local communities, observations of bird behaviours, and reflective insights significantly enrich these bird-watching experiences. These narratives offer powerful educational tools that foster a greater understanding and appreciation of cultural and ecological diversity. Bird watching thus becomes a transformative activity, bridging cultures, promoting sustainability, and deepening global environmental consciousness.

Conclusion

Bird symbolism remains an integral element of cultural identity worldwide, profoundly influencing humanity's relationship with nature. Through an extensive exploration of mythologies, folklore, philosophical insights, literary analyses, and global bird-watching narratives, we uncover the rich tapestry that connects humans and the natural world. Recognising the diverse cultural significances attached to birds enhances our ecological awareness, encouraging deeper empathy and more thoughtful interactions with the environment. Ultimately, embracing bird symbolism as a cultural lens fosters a greater sense of global unity and collective responsibility, reinforcing the essential interconnectedness between human societies and the ecosystems we inhabit.

Bird Watching Holidays & International Adventures

A Passport to Wonder

There is something quietly radical about travelling to watch birds. In an age of bucket lists and hyper-curated holidays, bird watching reminds people to slow down, to listen, and to look more deeply. It takes them not just across borders, but beyond themselves into marshes at dawn, mountain forests in silence, or endless savannahs where the air vibrates with life. To travel for birds is to carry curiosity as one's compass, to learn the names of creatures not for mastery, but for connection.

For many, these journeys begin with simple questions: What lives here that I have never seen before? What can this place teach me about attention, about presence, and about joy? Bird watching holidays are not escapes from life, but re-entries into it. They offer a return to the elemental: wind, water, birds, and a reminder that beauty does not obey our schedules.

In this chapter, we explore stories from birders who have travelled across Europe, into Africa, through the forests and beaches of Asia and the Americas, and even touched the ice edges of Antarctica. These are not just travel tales. They are meditations on the philosophy of movement, the psychology of discovery, and the ethics of entering other lives and landscapes.

United Kingdom: Between Familiarity and Surprise

Birders in the United Kingdom often speak of the quiet transformations that occur when familiar landscapes are seen through the lens of attentiveness. The UK's hedgerows, estuaries, and craggy coastlines, so often overlooked in daily life, become sites of revelation when observed with care. Even a city park, framed by binoculars, shifts from backdrop to stage, is a place where sparrows, starlings, and robins enact dramas of survival, song, and flight.

Many bird watchers return regularly to reserves like those in Norfolk and Suffolk, drawn by the vast skies and whispering reed beds. Among these reed beds, the booming call of a bittern may suddenly break the silence, which is a sound that seems to rise from the landscape itself. Bearded tits ping through the reeds like tiny bells, and marsh harriers glide above the waterways with a grace that feels both real and mythical.

In Scotland, along the still shores of highland lochs, patient birders wait through the cold, wrapped in wool and hope, for a glimpse of the elusive black-throated diver. When it appears, silent and spectral on the water, the reward is a moment of intimate witnessing and of a private miracle.

These experiences remind many that adventure does not always require distance. It requires patience. Presence. A capacity to be moved by what has been there all along. In the UK, the most significant surprises often lie at the edge of a local marsh or the bend of a quiet river, waiting, not for someone far-travelled, but for someone truly watching.

Reflection: Rediscovering the Known

Birding close to home reveals the depth of the everyday. It asks for less movement and more stillness. It challenges the assumption that wonder lies elsewhere. A hedge seen daily may still hold a secret. A bus stop can become a site of wildness.

Philosopher Simone Weil once wrote, *"Attention, taken to its highest degree, is the same thing as prayer."* Birders across Britain, tuning in to the subtlest shifts in feather or call, practise this form of attention. What they often discover is not just a more profound knowledge of birds, but a deepening of their capacity to see.

To watch birds close to home is to transform the familiar into the frontier. It turns the local into the lyrical. And in doing so, it reclaims the right to wonder as a return to a relationship with the world just outside the door.

Germany: The Everyday Made Extraordinary

Birders living in Germany often describe their relationship with the landscape as something built slowly rather than through itineraries, through rhythm. The country's rich ecological diversity, ranging from the flat, tidal expanses of the Wadden Sea to the mossy darkness of the Black Forest, and up into the rugged Alpine margins, creates a layered habitat mosaic, each region carrying its own seasonal tempo.

A favourite among many is the Lower Saxony Wadden Sea. There, knee-deep in the scent of brine and the pull of tidal rhythms, bird watchers observe vast flocks of waders: knot, dunlin, and oystercatcher that are wheeling above the flats. Their formations fold and unfold like living calligraphy across the sky.

The landscape is in constant motion, with the light shifting, the sea breathing in and out, and the birds responding with perfect choreography.

Others speak of urban marvels. Springtime in Bremen signals the return of swifts, their calls slicing the air above rooftops and looping through invisible corridors of sky. In autumn, redstarts pause in garden hedges and allotments. Even the ordinary, such as a supermarket car park or a tram stop, can become an unexpected stage for a vivid encounter.

Over time, these birders report a change not only in what they see, but also in how they perceive it. A bush that once seemed inert becomes alive with promise. Their perception deepens, season by season, informed by plumage and song, as well as by temperature, light, and sensation, and by the shift from observation to relationship that birding entails.

Reflection: The Familiar as a Frontier

In Germany, many people learn that birdwatching doesn't always require movement and sometimes requires immersion. And in that rootedness, a new kind of seeing is born. The same trail, walked repeatedly, becomes a mirror, reflecting the forest and the one walking through it. As perception sharpens, so does presence.

Philosopher Gaston Bachelard, in *The Poetics of Space*, describes the house as a universe where space is shaped by intimacy, memory, and attention. A favourite path, a city rooftop, or a quiet tree in the backyard can carry that same weight. Birding these places teaches that the familiar can be sacred.

Psychologically, this form of engagement provides a sense of security and stability. In times of personal dislocation or external uncertainty, these remembered birding grounds offer a sense of continuity. Redstarts return. Swifts carve the sky. And with them comes a sense of belonging, not just in space, but in time.

Birding becomes more than a hobby or a habit. It is a practice of orientation. A gentle defiance of distraction. A way of re-learning the world that is slower, intimate, and with reverence for the details that make it whole.

Africa: The Pulse of Life

Birders who travel to Africa often describe the experience in terms of scale and immersion as a visceral astonishment at the sheer vitality of colour, sound, and motion. No other place seems to prepare them for how alive the landscapes feel, how much memory ticks beneath the visible. In many accounts, the birds are a part of the environment and embody its spirit.

In the Okavango Delta of Botswana, early mornings are often spent drifting silently through papyrus channels in a mokoro, which is a traditional dugout canoe. Birders speak of being surrounded by layers of birdsong so complex and textured that it feels symphonic. Fish eagles call in antiphonal pairs across the sky, African jacanas tiptoe across lily pads with balletic grace, purple herons slide along the banks, necks poised like question marks. At every bend, there are bee-eaters, kingfishers, darters drying their wings in the gold of early light.

In South Africa, hides near waterholes offer extended hours of hushed observation. It is here that some have witnessed lilac-breasted rollers perform aerial acrobatics above a clearing, where their feathers flash turquoise, violet, and pink as they dive and tumble in courtship or play. They are often described as living jewels that are both wild and ornamental at the same time.

At Kenya's Lake Bogoria, birders speak in reverent tones of the flamingo flocks, numbering in the tens of thousands, sweeping across the shallows in choreographed waves, the lake itself shimmering pink. The movement is a spectacle, but is described as the rhythm of a heartbeat made visible.

And in quieter moments, dusk under an acacia tree might reveal a weaverbird weaving. There is no drama, and no performance, just patience and instinct, strand by strand, as the sun burns low behind it. Such moments are remembered for their stillness.

For many, the birds seen in Africa are ones they had only known from books or screens. But to be there to feel the dust, the heat, the insects buzzing, the slow swell of light is to be transformed. These are sightings, not encounters. The difference is crucial. Spectacle is observed from a distance. Presence requires participation.

Reflection: Reverence, Not Collection

Travelling through Africa often challenges the habits of Western birding culture, giving way to something more humble and authentic. There is a shift from acquiring to receiving. To witness a lilac-breasted roller, one cannot possess it but only be momentarily undone by it.

This shift opens the door to reverence. The landscapes are too vast, the lives too ancient, and the cycles too complex to be controlled. One waits. One listens. And let's go. In that surrender, something more profound is learned, a kind of ecological humility.

Philosopher Martin Buber's idea of the *"I–Thou"* relationship is often invoked here, where the bird is a being rather than an object, such that the encounter is relational. And in this way, birding becomes a form of ethical attention.

Psychologically, these moments bring coherence to a world of fractured attention, gathering the mind into a state of stillness. They awaken what is ancient in us of a hunter's focus, yes, but also a mystic's awe. They do not ask us to be quiet before it.

In Africa, birders return with softened eyes and a sense of wonder.

Asia: Between Temples and Tree Canopies

Birders exploring Asia often reflect on the striking juxtapositions the continent offers, with sacred spaces and wild spaces existing side by side, considered inseparable. One moment might bring the scent of incense from a nearby shrine, and the next, the flutter of wings in dense forest canopies. Birding in Asia rarely follows a straight line. It is more of a meandering through atmospheres, traditions, and layered ecologies where human presence and natural life speak in soft echoes.

In Japan, for example, travellers speak of winter journeys to Hokkaido, where snow rests heavily on black pine and the landscape hushes into a kind of spiritual stillness. At Lake Kussharo, volcanic springs steam into the cold air, and dozens of whooper swans gather. Their calls are long and trumpet-like, reverberating through the mist. Their stillness, their poise, and their silent reflections on the water create scenes that birders describe not just as beautiful, but as sacred, like watching a brushstroke in slow motion.

By contrast, birding in India is a cascade of sensation. At Keoladeo National Park in Rajasthan, cyclists weave through sun-baked trails lined with painted storks nesting in tangled trees. Parakeets screech as they dart between banyans, while kingfishers flash in and out of view over lotus-strewn canals. All of this unfolds amid a vibrant world of bells, markets, cricket games, and temple chants. In such places, the human and non-human are entangled.

Then there are the brackish, shifting landscapes of the Sundarbans, spanning India and Bangladesh. Here, birders speak of patience as an ethic. Many come hoping for the masked finfoot, which is rarely seen and often imagined; the *not-seeing* that becomes its form of presence. Every ripple, every rustle, feels charged. Birding here becomes a form of attunement to water, to shadow, to uncertainty.

Elsewhere, a barn owl might call from a temple ruin in Sri Lanka. A pair of hoopoes might feed quietly in a tea garden in Kerala. In the monsoon stillness, a drongo might unfurl its forked tail in a single gesture of silent drama. Across Asia, birds seem woven into stories that are half-remembered companions of saints, gods, and ghosts. Their presence lingers in both ecology and imagination.

Reflection: Layers of Seeing

Asia teaches birders that to see is to be immersed. It is not enough to catalogue a species because one must enter its world. In anthropological terms, this is a *"thick description"* of a witnessing of context, culture, ritual, sound, and scent.

A white-eye in a cherry tree is lovely. But beside a Shinto shrine, with incense rising and wind chimes dancing, and a woman bowing in reverence, it becomes something else. A portal. A symbol. A meeting place.

Birding in Asia is less about ticking names and more about receptivity. It is not curiosity alone that drives it, but rather its vulnerability, which leads to a willingness to dissolve the boundaries between self and other.

Philosophically, this echoes the Buddhist concept of interbeing, where no creature exists in isolation from others. The bird, the tree, the stone, the sky, and the observer are all parts of one moment. To witness a bird here is to participate in that wholeness.

Psychologically, birding in Asia can feel like a softening of the ego. The pace slows. The senses widen. The edges of experience blur. For many travellers, this shift offers healing. They come seeking birds and leave with stories of attention, texture, and having been transformed by the layered presence.

To bird in Asia is not to escape the world. It is to enter it more deeply of one feather, one footstep, and one prayer at a time.

The Americas: Wildness in Every Form

Across the Americas, from the rainforests of Costa Rica to the wind-scoured cliffs of Patagonia, birders often speak of being overwhelmed by abundance. The sheer scale of biodiversity, the riot of colour and song, the strangeness and splendour of life, all seem turned up, as if the continent itself insists on being noticed.

In Costa Rica, birding often begins with the raw call of howler monkeys and a cascade of birdsong spilling through the canopy. Mornings bring flashes of colour as blue-crowned motmots sit motionless in the shadows, their toucans outlined against the dawn sky, their oversized beaks improbably elegant, and hummingbirds zipping past like sparks. For many, the moment of awe arrives with the resplendent quetzal. Elusive and revered, this emerald-tailed beauty appears in cloud forests like a blessing.

One guide, pausing under fog-wrapped trees, whispered, *"Wait."* And then it seemed, trailing mist and myth alike.

In mangroves along the coast, scarlet macaws blaze across dark skies. Their passage feels elemental, like fire flaring into a storm.

Such moments are not just seen; they are felt.

Further north, in British Columbia, birders describe a shift in register. The mood is quieter and the light is gentler. Glacial lakes hold the stillness of long waits. Loons surface silently, their haunting calls curling over the water like a memory. In the Yukon, attention sharpens again. A gyrfalcon arcs through the cold, its flight controlled and effortless, a reminder of raw, muscular grace.

And then comes Patagonia. Vast, exposed, reverent. There, amid wind and stone, some have met the Andean condor, an ancient and wide-winged, rising with impossible ease on invisible thermals. It is not a bird so much as a symbol, a movement. A condor seen this way becomes an event, where one pauses time, reshapes scale, and stills the breath.

Reflection: Curiosity as a Compass

The Americas often require birders to surrender comfort in exchange for encounters. Journeys are not seamless. Things go wrong. Buses don't come. Maps lie. And birds fail to show. And yet the pursuit continues.

This kind of birding unhooks itself from certainty. It values curiosity over control. It invites a return to what some call a *"hunter-gatherer of wonder"* mindset by scanning not for presence, reading light and listening for tone, along with trusting intuition and letting go of the itinerary.

In this space, ambiguity becomes an ally. A trip without clear outcomes becomes a rich memory. A missed bird becomes a deeper patience. In letting go of the pressure to see, one begins to watch honestly.

Philosophically, this is an optimisation challenge. Modern life demands results. Birding in the Americas offers instead a relationship to land, to season, and to surprise. It asks: Can you show up without needing it to go your way?

Psychologically, this cultivates resilience. It grounds. It expands. And it reminds birders that they are not the centre, but part of a broader, wilder field. In this, they often find something more enduring than a list: a sense of being fully, briefly, and beautifully present.

Australia: The Strange and the Sublime

Among birders, Australia is often referred to as a place apart, a continent that seems to have written its evolutionary script. The land is old, its rhythms different, its rules unfamiliar. The birds reflect this strangeness and splendour of brilliance, bizarreity, and boldness. From the very first moment, travellers report a sense of disorientation and awe.

Cassowaries stalk the northern rainforests like spectral ancestors, part bird, part dinosaur, and part myth. Birders who glimpse them on shaded trails near Mission Beach describe a silence that follows, as if the encounter pauses time. Emus wander the inland plains like misplaced sentinels, their gait oddly comic, their presence commanding.

And then there are the lyrebirds. Deep in Victoria's forests, birders often hear them long before they are seen, as a symphony of chainsaw, camera shutter, and barking-dog mimicry. When finally visible, the bird's arched display is almost too theatrical to believe. With tail feathers fanned like a silver harp and movements executed with balletic control, the lyrebird performs not for an audience but for the forest itself.

In eucalyptus groves of New South Wales, the quietest mornings sometimes yield the most unforgettable scenes. A superb fairy-wren, electric blue and irrepressibly lively, flits among low brush, trailed by his companions. A kookaburra bursts into manic laughter. And then, as if conjured, a powerful owl emerges that is silent, immense, and gold-eyed. Its presence halts everything. Birders recall the world narrowing in that moment, as the forest becomes more vivid and more aware.

Further north in the Daintree, the elusive Victoria's riflebird enacts one of nature's most intricate rituals. Birders wait patiently beneath fruiting trees, sweat clinging to skin, with binoculars steady. When he arrives, shimmering black and green, the display begins with a trembling, iridescent dance beneath a shaft of jungle light. Those who witness it often describe the scene as an ancient theatre, elemental and precise.

Reflection: Wonder and the Unknown

Australia dismantles certainty. Even seasoned birders, with notebooks full and lifers ticked, find themselves humbled here. The birds defy easy classification. A song may sound artificial. A courtship display may blur the line between instinct and art. These creatures refuse to be domesticated by language.

This unpredictability requires a different kind of seeing with the open attention of the beginner rather than that of an expert. In Zen, this is called *shoshin*, a beginner's mind. Each encounter becomes a small rupture in what we think we know about each bird, a recalibration of perspective.

Emotionally, this creates space for transformation. Awe, by its very nature, decentres the self. Birders speak of encounters that quiet the ego, that remind them not of dominance over nature, but of their place within it.

There is also something intensely creative in these experiences. To watch a lyrebird dance, or a riflebird shimmer, is to witness a kind of non-human art that was not made for us, but capable of moving us. These birds are not just surviving; they are expressing.

In Australia, birding becomes more than a search. It becomes a surrender. Not a quest for control, but a witness to the wild. And in that surrender, something shifts. People return not just with sightings, but with widened eyes and softened hearts that have changed how they see rather than what they saw.

Antarctica: The Edge of Silence

Among those who make the long journey to Antarctica, there is often a shared sense of reverence upon arrival, recognising that they are about to step into something beyond their scale. On maps, the continent appears as a vast, white space, distant and unreachable. But for birders who cross the Drake Passage and witness its edges emerge from mist and sea, it becomes profoundly present.

What awaits is not spectacle, but essence. Ice. Silence. Light so clear it feels like the world has been scrubbed of its distractions. There are no trees. No buildings. No colours beyond blue, white, grey, and the occasional flash of plumage. Time slows into something elemental.

In this stark setting, the birds become the pulse of life. Colonies of Adélie penguins bustle across the ice, comic in posture but graceful beneath the surface. Their lives unfold in patterns ancient and unobserved. Birders speak of how perception shifts here, from what first seems awkward to what becomes perfect in context. The landscape teaches this re-seeing.

Emperor penguins stand in huddled constellations, their quiet flute-like calls carried on the wind. Their endurance, their instinctive care, seem beyond comprehension. There is no performance. No audience. Only life persists against indifference.

Skuas cut the air with sharp intent. Wilson's storm petrels skim the waves like ghosts stitched into water. And sometimes, when the air stills and the world narrows, a snow petrel may appear bright against the vastness, moving without sound or struggle. Those who have seen one describe it as an apparition of clarity. Birding in Antarctica is not about rarity. It is about a relationship. It is about learning how to be still enough to witness what does not need us.

Reflection: Stillness as Revelation

What Antarctica offers is a vast, patient, and utterly still landscape. It strips away distractions like nothing else, and in return, it demands nothing but your attention. And in that attentive silence, something internal begins to settle.

Birders speak of how the continent recalibrates them. There is no signal. No timeline. No expectation of entertainment. The scaffolding of modern identity, centred on productivity, performance, and pace, falls away. What remains is presence.

The birds here are not background. They are emissaries of another scale. They do not care if they are seen. They move by older logics of current, temperature, season, and instinct. To watch them is to glimpse a form of existence that is whole without narrative.

Philosophically, Antarctica confronts the observer with the sublime. Not beauty, exactly, but vastness beyond understanding. As Kant noted, the sublime does not comfort. Instead, it unsettles, then elevates. And in that elevation, one remembers how small and how lucky we are.

Psychologically, the impact lingers. Birders describe a softness that follows them home to a quieter pace, with a greater tolerance for silence, and a willingness to be with what is unresolved.

Something inside them remembers the snow petrel. Remembers the wind. Remembers how to listen.

To journey to Antarctica is to be reminded of where seeing begins in the stillness, in the humility, and in awe.

Final Reflection: Travel as Transformation

Across continents, climates, and cultures, birdwatching has never been about birds alone. It has always been about something more elemental, about how people move through the world, how they pay attention, and how they allow themselves to be changed by what they witness.

Each journey begins with a question: What lives here that has never been seen before? But beneath that question often lies another: Who might I become through this seeing?

In the United Kingdom, birders learn that wonder doesn't require distance or only presence. That the familiar, when seen with care, becomes a frontier.

In Germany, the magic lies in repetition. Returning to the same place with new eyes reveals that slowness is a form of intimacy. Africa teaches reverence. It invites birders to enter other ecologies with humility, not as collectors, but as guests.

Asia reminds us that birds do not live apart from human life, but within it. That beauty often rests in context as much as in colour. The Americas reward those who follow curiosity beyond their comfort zone. Here, birding becomes a way to embrace unpredictability, to find joy in what is unplanned.

Australia reawakens awe. It unsettles assumptions and, in doing so, expands the imagination of what nature can be.

Antarctica gives stillness. A silence so complete that even the air seems to listen, and in that silence, something realigns within.

Taken together, these journeys are not about seeing more birds. They are about seeing differently. About loosening the grip of control and letting the world reveal itself, not as something to consume, but as something to relate to.

Bird watching holidays are not escapes. They are returns.

Returns to the senses, after too much abstraction. Returns to the earth after too much screenlight. Return to each other after too much separation.

They remind us that we are not separate from the natural world, but expressions of it, with eyes that can witness, hearts that can open, and feet that can follow feathered guides into new ways of being.

In the end, travellers do not come back with souvenirs. They come back with stories, with perspectives shifted, and with inner landscapes subtly reshaped by outer ones.

To watch a bird is to witness a mystery made visible. To follow birds across borders is to say yes, again and again, to curiosity, to fragility, and to connection. And perhaps, most profoundly, to change.

Citizen Science & Environmental Awareness

The Power of Many

A single bird watcher on a quiet path may seem to be a solitary figure with binoculars in hand, and a notebook tucked in a pocket or an app open on a phone. Yet this solitary act, multiplied by thousands, indeed millions, forms one of the most significant grassroots scientific movements in human history. Bird watching has evolved from a pastime into a vital engine for data, awareness, and conservation. From backyard feeders in the UK to rainforest canopies in Brazil, bird watchers have emerged as silent sentinels of the planet's health.

This chapter examines how bird watching has evolved into a vital tool for citizen science and its implications for the future of our shared environment. It explores the philosophical roots of participation, celebrates success stories from around the world, and confronts the ethical consequences of gaining a deeper understanding of our fragile ecosystems. Above all, it is a chapter about agency, of how we, through the simple act of noticing, become guardians of life.

Birds as Data: A Democratic Science

Long before the term *"citizen science"* gained traction, bird watchers were already laying the groundwork for its principles. In the 19th century, amateur naturalists contributed species observations to ornithological societies, often becoming the primary recorders of avian life. In 1900, Frank M. Chapman of the Audubon Society proposed a new tradition of the Christmas Bird Count. Instead of the customary holiday hunt, participants would count and report birds. Over a century later, this annual count continues across North America and beyond, yielding one of the most extensive longitudinal datasets on avian populations.

Birds are particularly well-suited to citizen science. They are mobile, visible, vocal, and responsive to environmental changes. The keen eyes and ears of birders, who are often more numerous and widespread than professional scientists who have enabled the tracking of migration patterns, identification of population declines, and even the detection of early signs of climate change.

Importantly, this form of science is democratic. It lowers the threshold of entry to the realm of data collection and analysis. One does not need to be a professional to make a meaningful contribution. The boundaries between experts and enthusiasts blur as checklists become datasets and sightings inform conservation policy.

What makes this even more powerful is its intergenerational nature. Children, parents, and grandparents can observe and record together, building both family bonds and long-term awareness. Even casual observations, like those from a window feeder, accumulate over time to form rich ecological records.

eBird and the Digital Revolution

If early citizen science was built on notepads and letters, the 21st century has given it wings through technology. The launch of eBird by the Cornell Lab of Ornithology in 2002 revolutionised bird watching and environmental data collection. With a few taps on a smartphone, users can log sightings, upload photos or audio recordings, and contribute to a centralised global database. As of 2025, eBird boasts over a billion observations from more than 700,000 contributors worldwide.

This sheer volume of data has enabled breakthroughs in avian science. Real-time migration maps, heatmaps of bird activity, and predictive models of species decline are now accessible not only to scientists but to anyone with an internet connection. Researchers use eBird data to track shifts in species ranges due to climate change, understand the effects of urbanisation, and inform land-use decisions.

The influence of this technology extends beyond science as it transforms the personal experience of bird-watching. For many, the ability to instantly contribute to a larger cause adds depth to each outing. It fosters a sense of connection to a broader community and to the Earth itself. A bird seen is a voice heard, and a voice heard is a life counted.

Yet eBird is more than a tool. It is a philosophy that knowledge grows through openness and collaboration. It invites us to be co-authors in the story of Earth's biodiversity. It exemplifies the potential of distributed intelligence, where each sighting, no matter how small, becomes part of a planetary narrative.

The digital age has made participation easier, but it has also made it more meaningful. Knowing that one's observation of a marsh harrier in East Anglia or a sunbird in Kenya might help protect wetlands or forests across the globe imbues the act with weight. Observation becomes stewardship.

Participation in Philosophy

Citizen science is more than about data; it is about a shift in worldview. It challenges the passive consumer model of environmentalism, where one donates, reads, or laments, and replaces it with active engagement. Watching, noticing, and recording are radical acts in a culture of distraction.

To observe a bird is to step into an ancient relationship. Humans have watched birds for millennia, for signs of weather, omens, food sources, or spiritual guidance. Today, this watching takes on new urgency. In an age of mass extinction and ecological crisis, observation becomes a form of solidarity.

The philosopher Arne Næss, the father of Deep Ecology, argued that identification with nature, feeling oneself part of the living world, is essential for genuine ecological action. Bird watching fosters such identification. The joy of recognising a bird's call, the quiet pride in adding a new species to a personal list, and the sorrow of hearing that a once-common bird is now rare are the roots of ethical response.

Rachel Carson, too, reminds us in *Silent Spring* that the real danger is not only what poisons the earth but what deadens our awareness. In contrast, citizen science keeps us awake. It makes us witnesses. Participation is not only ethical, but also existential. In an age where digital alienation, consumer overload, and environmental despair erode our sense of agency, the act of taking a walk and noticing becomes revolutionary. It anchors us in the present, restores our attention spans, and reaffirms our connection to something greater than ourselves.

Stories of Impact: Global Citizen Science

Around the world, bird watchers are changing the conservation landscape. In the UK, the Royal Society for the Protection of Birds (RSPB) organises the annual Big Garden Birdwatch. Launched in 1979, it now involves over half a million participants each year, making it the world's largest wildlife survey. The data inform national policy and help detect long-term trends in species such as the house sparrow and starling.

In South America, local birders working with BirdLife International have helped protect habitats critical to migratory birds and endangered species. In Ecuador, the discovery of new hummingbird populations by amateur ornithologists led to the establishment of new protected areas, or reserves.

In India, the State of India's Birds report, based on millions of citizen records, has highlighted sharp declines in species such as the Indian vulture, raising alarms that have shaped national conservation priorities.

In Kenya, community-based monitoring has supported the conservation of wetlands vital to the survival of flamingo populations. In Indonesia, villagers trained to monitor hornbill nests have become central actors in preserving forest biodiversity.

In the United States, the Great Backyard Bird Count and the Breeding Bird Survey combine data from thousands of participants to inform land management strategies and habitat restoration efforts. Meanwhile, in Australia, citizen science has contributed to awareness campaigns on the plight of the Carnaby's black cockatoo, leading to policy changes to address deforestation.

These stories share a common thread: the merger of local observation with global impact. They demonstrate how citizen science can be inclusive, empowering, and scalable. Additionally, they reveal a conservation model that respects local knowledge and foregrounds community involvement.

The Ecology of Community: Building Networks of Care

One of the most inspiring aspects of citizen science is how it fosters relationships between people and birds, as well as among people themselves. Bird watching may begin as a personal interest, but it often evolves into a form of community-building. Walks become shared experiences. Rare sightings prompt conversations among strangers. Online forums, birding clubs, and local meetups become spaces where knowledge, curiosity, and affection for nature are exchanged freely.

These communities operate on principles that echo ecological thinking: diversity, reciprocity, and balance. Experienced birders often mentor novices. Younger participants bring digital skills and enthusiasm. Older generations offer patient insight and deep familiarity with local landscapes. Together, they form networks of care.

Community science projects go even further. In some towns, birding events coincide with habitat restoration efforts. Schools partner with nature centres to create bird-friendly gardens. Libraries host identification workshops. Public parks are equipped with bird hides and interpretive signs thanks to collective advocacy. These hobbyist gatherings are civic movements grounded in stewardship.

Furthermore, watching together often creates emotional connections that extend beyond the birds themselves. Grieving the decline of a species can foster a sense of shared loss and solidarity, evoking a profound sense of connection and empathy. Celebrating the return of a migratory flock can inspire a shared understanding of joy. The emotional texture of birding is thick with memory, story, and place. It is from this texture that a culture of care arises, one that links observation to action.

The community aspect also opens doors to inclusivity and justice. Historically, access to green space and environmental education has been uneven, shaped by class, race, and geography. The citizen science model, with its low barriers to entry and emphasis on participation over credentialism, presents a promising approach.

Initiatives that bring binoculars and mentorship to inner-city schools, or that collaborate with Indigenous communities to recover traditional ecological knowledge, reflect a broader truth. Everyone has a role to play in conservation, and every voice matters in the chorus.

By nurturing this community ecology, birdwatching becomes a culture. And culture, in its most potent form, changes hearts, minds, and systems.

A Global Chorus

The image of the lone bird watcher is misleading. Bird watching is a communal act, even when done in solitude. Each checklist, each call identified, each photograph uploaded is a note in a global chorus that sings of beauty, but also of fragility, urgency, and hope.

In that chorus, we find an ethic as an invitation to look toward. To let the joy of watching birds become the seed of environmental action. To let wonder grow into wisdom. And to understand that in the end, citizen science is about birds just as much as it is about us.

The birds are speaking. Our job is to listen, to learn, and to ensure that their songs do not fall silent.

The Ethics of Seeing

With knowledge comes responsibility. As bird watchers gather more data and gain more insight, the ethical landscape becomes more complex. Should a rare nesting site be made public if it risks disturbance? What happens when enthusiastic birders flood a sensitive area, driven by the hope of a sighting?

The ethics of bird watching extend beyond the individual to the collective. Birders must navigate questions of access, privilege, and harm. Who gets to watch, where, and how? How do we ensure that the joy of observation does not come at the expense of the observed?

Some organisations have responded with codes of conduct that include guidelines for maintaining a respectful distance, preserving habitats, and implementing data-sharing protocols to protect vulnerable species. However, deeper than rules lies the cultivation of awareness: an ethic of attentiveness, humility, and care.

We must also consider the broader environmental implications. Driving long distances to see a rare bird may seem harmless, but it cumulatively contributes to carbon emissions. Similarly, using playback calls to lure birds for photos may disturb their natural behaviour. Responsible birding means thinking about what we do, but how and why.

Environmental awareness, when genuine, transforms into a sense of duty as a quiet calling. One that recognises that each sighting is also a gift, and that such gifts carry the weight of guardianship.

The Future of Citizen Science

The tools of citizen science are evolving. Acoustic monitoring and AI-driven species recognition are opening new frontiers. Remote sensors, community apps, and data visualisation platforms allow even greater integration between individuals and institutions.

Imagine a future in which city-dwelling children use wearable devices that automatically record bird calls during walks to school, contributing passively yet powerfully to large ecological databases. Or a scenario where local indigenous knowledge is encoded and preserved through partnerships with scientific bodies, ensuring that tradition informs technology.

But technology alone is not enough. The future of citizen science depends on participation. It needs schools to teach observation as a form of ecological literacy. It requires platforms that welcome diversity in species and in people. It needs to amplify voices from underrepresented regions and ensure that global data includes the global South.

Crucially, it must resist the temptation to replace presence with proxies. While satellite data and machine learning are powerful tools, there is no substitute for the human gaze and the stories it conveys. Bird watching reminds us that to protect something, we must first fall in love with it. And love begins with looking.

The rise of youth movements in climate and biodiversity action is a hopeful sign. Young people around the world are picking up binoculars, joining bioblitzes, and using technology to amplify their voices. They are showing that citizenship in the age of ecological crisis means active participation, all without waiting for permission to start.

A Global Chorus

The image of the lone birdwatcher can be misleading because birdwatching is a communal act, even when done in solitude. Each checklist, each call identified, each photograph uploaded is a note in a global chorus. A chorus that sings not only of beauty, but of fragility, of urgency, of hope.

In that chorus, and as I have said before, we find that ethic is the invitation that we don't look away. Instead, we look forward by letting the joy of watching birds become the seed of environmental action, allowing wonder to grow into wisdom, and understanding that, in the end, citizen science is not just about birds; it is about us.

The birds are speaking. Our job is to listen, to learn, and to ensure that their songs do not fall silent.

Inclusivity & Accessibility in Bird Watching

The Joy of Birds for All

Bird watching, at its core, appears to be one of the most democratic hobbies. There are no entry fees to gaze at the sky, no qualifications needed to admire the plumage of a wren or follow the looping dive of a swift. In theory, anyone with a spark of curiosity and a willingness to slow down can participate. Yet, in practice, access to the joys of birding is not always evenly distributed. Barriers related to age, ability, socioeconomic background, and cultural inclusion mean that some people are less likely to find their place in this world of feathers and song.

This chapter explores both the challenges and the triumphs of stories of individuals and communities who defy limitations and find connection in nature. It considers how the philosophy of equality and shared access to beauty underpins ethical bird watching, and how the act of observation itself can deepen empathy, understanding, and a commitment to diversity.

Ultimately, this chapter celebrates the idea that bird watching can become inclusive in theory and welcoming in practice.

Age as an Access Barrier

Inclusivity in bird watching must begin with recognising the very different ways age can shape access. For children and teenagers, birding can be perceived as too quiet, too solitary, or lacking the instant gratification common in digital entertainment. Unless a child has a bird-loving parent, teacher, or local guide, they may never think to look skyward and wonder who is singing. Schools often prioritise sports or traditional science education over nature-based learning, and birding opportunities are not evenly distributed.

At the other end of the spectrum, older adults may find themselves physically limited. Arthritis, reduced mobility, and chronic illness can make long walks through uneven terrain difficult or impossible. Yet, the rise of digital tools, including birding apps, online ID guides, and citizen science platforms, can also pose a barrier for those who are less comfortable with smartphones or computers.

And yet, some of the most devoted birders are in their seventies and eighties. One memorable encounter took place in a small English village, where I met Harold, an elderly man using a mobility scooter to patrol the hedgerows at dawn. He carried a lightweight pair of binoculars in one hand and a thermos of tea in the other. He couldn't walk more than a few steps unaided, but his daily route was carefully chosen down a narrow lane with robins, wrens, and blue tits almost guaranteed. *"They keep me alive,"* he said plainly. *"Every morning, I need to see who's still around. They don't care how old I am. They sing anyway."*

Age inclusivity also requires intergenerational dialogue, recognising that birding thrives when stories and knowledge are passed down from one generation to the next. Too often, birding clubs are seen as ageing institutions, with few young members and a culture that may feel rigid or unwelcoming to newcomers. Mentorship programmes, school outreach, and family bird walks are ways to begin bridging that gap, creating spaces where the wisdom of experience meets the fresh curiosity of youth.

Ability and the Right to Observe

For individuals living with physical or cognitive disabilities, bird watching can present challenges, but also unexpected joys. Many bird hides, trails, and nature reserves remain inaccessible. Steps, narrow doorways, lack of signage, or unpaved paths can render beautiful areas off-limits to wheelchair users or those with reduced vision.

Yet innovation and empathy are shifting the landscape. Adaptive birding equipment, including binocular harnesses, voice-activated field guides, and guided experiences tailored to specific needs, is gaining popularity. Some organisations now offer birding walks specifically designed for neurodiverse participants, including individuals with autism or sensory processing differences. These events typically emphasise routine, reduced stimulation, and gentle engagement, and are often co-led by neurodivergent guides.

A particularly moving example comes from a group in southern Germany offering *"birding by ear"* walks for blind and visually impaired participants. Rather than focusing on plumage, these walks train participants to identify calls, rhythms, and locations by sound. One participant described the joy of hearing a blackcap trill for the first time and knowing exactly what it was. *"It was like a voice I'd always known but never named."*

The conversation around accessibility also extends to mental health. For individuals struggling with anxiety, PTSD, or depression, traditional group activities may feel overwhelming.

Bird watching, especially when adapted to solo or small-group formats, offers a powerful alternative. The quiet, the rhythm, and the contact with the non-verbal world can all contribute to healing. Inclusive birding should therefore also be trauma-informed, offering choices that are sensitive to overwhelm and no pressure to perform.

Socioeconomic Inequality

Bird watching is often imagined as low-cost or free, but that masks a more profound truth: meaningful access requires time, money, and proximity to nature. A decent pair of binoculars, field guides, waterproof clothing, and transport to green areas are often unaffordable luxuries for those living paycheck to paycheck.

Urban environments, particularly in underserved areas, often lack safe and accessible green spaces. For many young people growing up in housing estates or inner-city flats, birds are either invisible or viewed as background noise. Add to this the feeling that birding is an activity for the privileged or educated, and a powerful form of self-exclusion can take hold.

Representation also matters. In the United States, movements like *"Birding While Black"* have drawn attention to the racism and suspicion experienced by some birders of colour. In Europe, birding communities remain overwhelmingly white and middle-class. Without active efforts to include and welcome marginalised communities, these patterns are likely to persist.

Practical solutions exist, such as community-run optics libraries (where people can borrow binoculars like books), subsidised travel to reserves, and mentorship schemes that pair experienced birders with newcomers. Public libraries could double as hubs for local bird clubs. But these efforts must be part of a larger cultural shift that redefines birdwatching not as a rarefied hobby but as a birthright.

Listening in the Dark: Maria's Story

Maria lost her vision in her twenties due to a degenerative condition. A lifelong lover of nature, she mourned what she thought was the end of her ability to connect with birds. But after attending a soundscape workshop in the Netherlands, she began to retrain her senses. Using parabolic microphones and guided tapes, Maria became adept at identifying dozens of birds by ear. Today, she leads her sound walks. *"Birding is about attention, not sight,"* she explains. *"And attention is something I have in abundance."* She describes birding as her form of meditation, as a daily immersion in a world of rhythm and melody.

Finding Wings: Jamal's Story

Jamal grew up in a high-rise block in London. His school rarely took students outdoors, and his exposure to wildlife was limited to pigeons and the occasional fox. But when a local charity offered an after-school programme on urban nature, Jamal signed up out of curiosity. On their first field trip, he saw a green woodpecker and was hooked.

Now eighteen, Jamal runs a youth birding blog and organises free walks for local children. *"I didn't know birds could be so full of personality,"* he writes. *"No one ever told me they could be mine, too."*

A Quiet Refuge: Khaled's Story

Khaled, a Syrian refugee living in Germany, arrived traumatised and isolated. Language barriers and loss of community left him withdrawn. One day, a social worker invited him on a walk-through through a nearby park. They spotted a heron, and Khaled paused. *"We have birds like that back home,"* he said softly.

The following week, he came back with a borrowed pair of binoculars. Over time, bird watching became a way to ground himself in the present. He joined a local birding group, found a shared language in gestures and pointing, and gradually rebuilt his confidence.

The Power of Community

In cities around the world, grassroots initiatives are reclaiming birding as a community act. Pop-up bird walks in Berlin's immigrant neighbourhoods, second-hand binocular donation drives, and multilingual signage in urban parks are helping to expand the circle. Volunteers who offer lifts to reserves or birders who mentor others online are part of a quiet movement toward inclusion.

Often, these stories don't make headlines. But each shared moment, when a child sees their first swan, an older person identifies a call from memory and adds to the collective richness of bird-watching.

Mentorship and Belonging

Mentorship plays a vital role in building bridges. Experienced birders who invite newcomers, without pressure, jargon, or superiority, create openings for transformation. When someone is shown a bird through another's lens, both people change.

One such story comes from Carla, a retired teacher who began organising monthly *"walk-and-wonder"* sessions for mothers and children in her neighbourhood. *"I realised I didn't want to be alone anymore,"* she said. *"So, I opened it up. And they came."*

Nature as Commons

The question of who has access to nature is a deeply philosophical one. Thinkers from Rousseau to Thoreau have argued that the natural world belongs to no one, yet to everyone. In modern times, Aldo Leopold's land ethic and Arne Næss's deep ecology have emphasised seeing nature not as a resource, but as a community to which we belong.

This view places an ethical obligation on society to ensure that beauty, wildness, and silence are not privileges of the few. If bird watching fosters joy, calm, and reflection, then its gates should not be hidden behind walls of wealth, ability, or cultural familiarity.

Equality Through Shared Wonder

Bird watching can be a great leveller. In a field or forest, all eyes turn skyward. The kingfisher doesn't care who is watching. The moment of awe, that intake of breath when a bird appears, is democratic. It belongs to whoever is paying attention.

And yet, equality of experience demands equity of access. It is not enough to say that the woods are free if there's no bus to reach them. It is not enough to say that birds are visible if you cannot afford glasses. The philosophy of shared wonder calls for practical actions, such as paths, benches, guides, and invitations.

Inclusivity Beyond Humans

Birds are not our possessions. They are our neighbours, fellow travellers, and teachers. Watching them with care and respect invites us into a more humble relationship with the world. In this way, inclusive bird watching is about stepping back from human-centred thinking.

To watch a flock wheel over the sea is to see something ancient, indifferent, and utterly beautiful. It serves as a reminder that belonging is not something to be earned; it is given. It simply is.

Empathy and Perspective-Taking

Birders are trained to focus their attention by noticing subtle differences, exercising patience, and adapting their expectations. These are also the skills of empathy. To be inclusive as a birder is to cultivate the capacity to imagine someone else's way of seeing.

The child who hears better than she sees, the man who counts feathers instead of species, the woman who can't leave her flat but watches birds from her window, are all part of the story. Expanding inclusion means expanding the ways we understand observation itself.

Understanding and Belonging

Psychologists consider *"belonging"* a fundamental human need. Inclusive birding groups, those that welcome questions, explain without condescension, and celebrate enthusiasm while offering a kind of psychological safety.

This matters more than we often realise. For many, joining a birding group may be the first time they feel part of something without needing to compete, perform, or defend their presence. Birding becomes more than just a hobby; it becomes a place to land.

Celebrating Diversity

The bird world is a riot of diversity of iridescent feathers, odd calls, and unusual behaviours. Birders learn early that difference is not a defect. The same principle can also apply to human communities.

Inclusive birding groups often reflect this natural diversity. Elderly and young, introverted and gregarious, as well as the experienced and the new, comprise a diverse group of birders that can be a strength when stories are shared, knowledge grows, and friendships form across unexpected boundaries.

Transformative Encounters

Sometimes, a single moment can change everything. A bird is landing near someone who has never noticed birds before. A rare sighting witnessed with others. A conversation in a hide between strangers who become friends.

Such moments are not trivial. They are flashes of grace. In an increasingly fragmented world, bird watching can be a place of reconnection, not only with nature but also with one another.

A Flock of All Kinds

To make bird watching truly inclusive is to commit to the idea that joy should be for everyone. That silence, beauty, and curiosity are not luxuries but needs. That we each carry something of value into the field.

The future of bird watching depends not just on preserving habitats, but also on expanding hearts, building trails that everyone can walk, hosting groups that everyone can join, and telling stories that reflect the diverse lives of many people.

Please picture this: a small group is gathered by a still lake. A girl in a wheelchair, an elderly man with a hearing aid, a refugee with quiet eyes, and a child pointing excitedly. They are all watching the same heron lift slowly into the sky. No one speaks. They don't need to.

In that moment, they are one flock. And the bird does not ask who they are.

Humour, Joy, and Quirky Encounters

"The earth laughs in flowers," wrote Ralph Waldo Emerson, but perhaps it also chuckles in birdsong. Amid the silence of the woods or the stillness of a marsh, laughter and lightness often arrive uninvited, like a pheasant bursting from the undergrowth at just the wrong moment or a birdwatcher slipping in mud while trying to appear dignified. In this chapter, we celebrate the comedic, joyful, and eccentric aspects of bird watching. Behind every serious observer lies a person who, at least once, laughed so hard their binoculars fogged up.

A World of Bird-Induced Humour

Our journey begins with a classic bird-watching blunder: mistaking a rogue plastic bag for a rare bird. I recall a breezy day along the Northumberland coast when someone in our group let out an excited cry: *"Look! A snowy owl!"* Every scope and binocular turned, hearts racing. There it was, stark white, fluttering gently in the grass... only to lift suddenly and drift across the field, revealing itself to be a Tesco carrier bag. The silence that followed was broken only by a child's quiet giggle, then by a collective, sheepish laugh.

Bird watching, despite its image of tranquil reverence, is full of moments like this. Misidentifications are almost a rite of passage. A friend once called me at sunrise from a hide in Norfolk, whispering urgently that she had spotted a *"crimson-breasted warbler."* There is no such bird. What she had seen, in dim morning light, was a robin in front of a red Coca-Cola can.

Birds with Personality: The Comedians of the Sky

Birds themselves are often the unwitting performers in our outdoor theatre. Consider the magpie that is half prankster, half philosopher. I once watched a pair take turns bouncing on a trampoline in a suburban garden. Each bird would leap into the centre, then bounce clumsily, wings flailing, before being launched into the air. They returned, again and again, cackling in their strange corvid way.

The puffin, with its comical waddle and clumsy landings, often seems like a living cartoon. On the Farne Islands, a friend witnessed one attempt to land, which miscalculated and resulted in a tumble into a group of sunbathing seals. The seals barely blinked. The puffin, dignity wounded, picked itself up and strutted off, as though nothing had happened.

But not all comic birds are colourful or exotic. The humble pigeon, for instance, has provided me with more accidental humour than I care to admit. Once, on a city-centre walk with a new birding friend, I raised my binoculars dramatically to inspect what I insisted was *"an oddly pale dove."* It was a plastic owl decoy perched on a window ledge. I tried to salvage my dignity by discussing predator deterrence theory, but the damage was done.

Birds don't mean to be funny, but they remind us how unserious the world can be when we let it.

The Psychology of Laughter in the Wild

What makes these moments so delightful? Psychologically, humour in nature serves as an emotional release. Bird watching often requires stillness, patience, and quiet, as a form of self-restraint. When something unexpected happens, it breaks the tension. It's as if nature is permitting us to let go.

In a more profound sense, humour in wild places has a balancing effect. Many birders pursue *"lifers"* - *birds seen for the first time - with a seriousness that borders* on obsession. Hours, sometimes days, are spent chasing a rare warbler or staking out a shy species.

The tension builds.

And then, your tripod collapses in a puddle. A swan honks mid-photo and startles you. A cow wanders up behind you and nudges your scope. These moments reframe the whole experience.

They shake us from our self-importance and return us to what positive psychologists call *'flow,'* a state of being fully immersed in the moment, where delight and failure are both part of the game.

Philosopher Henri Bergson argued that humour comes from *"the mechanical encrusted upon the living"* rigid patterns appearing where spontaneity is expected. Many bird behaviours are comic precisely because they look accidental, human-like, or absurdly ill-timed. A bird slipping from a perch, chasing its tail, or appearing utterly confused by a mirror are all things that resemble us.

And in these moments, we realise birding isn't about success. It's about being there awkwardly, humanly, and joyfully present.

Joyful Memories in the Field

Bird watching with others often creates a special camaraderie, especially in those moments when the birds make fools of us all. I recall a weekend trip with our local bird club, when we all rose at 4 a.m. for a supposed sighting of a rare green heron. We stood, half-awake, staring at reeds, not saying a word. One member leaned over and whispered, *"This better not be another duck."* Just then, a mallard exploded from the reeds, honking madly. The group burst into laughter.

It *was* just another duck.

Some of the fondest birding memories are full of mishaps. On one weekend in Wales, a colleague forgot to pack lunch in the car. With no food for hours and no shop nearby, we resorted to splitting a single cereal bar into six pieces. Spirits were low until a red kite flew overhead, looping and gliding as if putting on a private show. *"It's trying to find the rest of our lunch,"* someone quipped. Laughter bloomed. Hunger forgotten. The bird had fed us something else entirely.

Another time, a friend joined a group walk led by a famously strict ornithologist. He expected silence and discipline. But about twenty minutes in, someone's ringtone blared: *"Surfin' Bird"* by The Trashmen. The group dissolved. Even the stern leader cracked a smile. *"Well,"* he said, *"at least it's bird-themed."*

Quirky Behaviour: Birds as Tricksters

Some birds seem to have a sense of mischief, or at least that's how we interpret their actions, with jays hiding other birds 'food caches. Crows are dropping nuts onto roads and waiting for cars to crack them open. Gulls are stealing sandwiches with surgical precision. The line between animal instinct and cleverness sometimes feels blurred.

In Shetland, another spotter witnessed a raven steal a fisherman's mobile phone. It dropped it onto a cliff, then flew away, seemingly proud. In Australia, bowerbirds decorate their *"bowers"* with blue bottle caps, pens, and even toy cars, as nature's collectors, but with eccentric taste. There's joy in this strangeness, a kind of alien intelligence that delights in puzzles, colour, and games.

The jackdaw, often overlooked, has a stare worthy of a Shakespearean villain and a sense of humour to match. One winter, I watched one approach a picnic bench. It paused, as if thinking. Then it stole a packet of crisps not by pecking, but by pulling the edge with its claw like a tiny raccoon. It perched on the bench, opened the bag, and dropped a crisp to the ground, as if sharing.

And who could ignore the grebes, with their elaborate courtship dances? What begins as a ritual becomes comic through repetition. At a distance, it looked like two birds performing a synchronised swimming routine choreographed by someone with a love for slapstick.

These behaviours reveal something beautiful about nature, too: rhythm, pattern, and surprise. In trying to decode them, we sometimes laugh at ourselves for even trying.

Children and the Joy of Seeing Differently

Children bring a unique lens to bird watching, one coloured by wonder, mischief, and delightful confusion.

My neighbour's nephew once exclaimed that she saw a *"stripy penguin"* in the garden. It was a great tit. But to her, its yellow chest and bold patterns felt exotic. *"It's wearing a jumper,"* she insisted. Who are we to disagree?

Kids also lack the filter that stops adults from expressing joy openly. They cheer. They talk to birds. They name them. One child in a family would walk and name every robin they saw *"Steven."* When I asked why, he shrugged and said, *"They just look like Stevens."*

Their questions are often funnier than the birds themselves:
- *"Do owls ever wear sunglasses?"*
- *"Do birds have birthdays?"*
- *"Why don't birds need to wee?"*

You may not have answers, but the laughter is enough.

Family Follies and Joyful Disasters

Family bird watching trips are their genre of comedy. One Easter, we went to Norfolk and met up with friends. They're not birders, but they're polite enough to pretend. After an hour, he turned to me and said, *"Do they do anything else other than flap about?"*

Then, as if on cue, a lapwing performed its mad sky dance, tumbling and shrieking. He nodded, impressed. *"Right, now that's a show."*

There was a time when we took a trip to a well-known kingfisher site. We were excited with binoculars ready, and hours passed, but there was no bird. Then, just as we were leaving, a sudden flash of blue darted past. *"There it is!"* someone shouted. We all turned, only to see a child's balloon drifting through the trees. Blue, shiny, kingfisher-shaped. Laughter erupted, tinged with disappointment, but also with a weird joy. The anticipation had united us.

Another time, a larger-than-life family arrived at a reserve with a foldable stool, a tartan flask, and a novel. *"Let me know when something big flies past,"* the mother said. In the end, she had the best day of all, resting in the sun, sipping tea, and occasionally clapping when others got excited.

Philosophical Joy: Laughter as Liberation

From a philosophical perspective, joy and humour in nature are liberating. Friedrich Nietzsche once described laughter as *"a devil who has leapt over everything,"* breaking rules and hierarchies. In bird watching, where observation is often reverent and hierarchical (experts vs. beginners, to rare vs. common), laughter levels the field.

The French philosopher Georges Bataille once said, *"Laughter is a kind of communion, a return to the sacred through rupture."* That rupture, which is a break in seriousness, a surprise of the ridiculous, is often what restores our sense of belonging in nature.

It reminds us we're part of nature, not outside it. When we laugh at a gull stealing chips or a wren bouncing like a tennis ball, we are laughing at ourselves, too, at our expectations, our habits, our need for control.

Joy also connects us to a sense of gratitude. As Thich Nhat Hanh wrote, *"Sometimes your joy is the source of your smile, but sometimes your smile can be the source of your joy."* In bird watching, smiling and laughter are invitations to a state of presence. There are ways of noticing.

The Art of Being Silly Outdoors

There's an art to silliness. We lose it in adulthood, having been trained instead to perform competently. But in the field with binoculars fogged, scopes tumbling, and sandwiches eaten by dogs, that pretence quickly falls away.

Birding permits us to play. To wear absurd hats. To crawl through bushes. To mimic birdsong poorly. During one group outing, we attempted to imitate the calls of a tawny owl. Instead, we summoned an irate farmer who thought we were hooligans. The birds didn't come, but the memory stayed.

Other birders have even made up games: who can spot the *"grumpiest gull"?* Who can invent the best alternate names for familiar birds? (After listening to them, my favourites include *"angry marsh banana"* for the bittern and *"snob duck"* for the mandarin).

Silliness has a secret power. It renews attention. It refreshes tired eyes and ears. And it brings people together in quiet, yet meaningful ways. A shared smirk in a hide or a whispered joke during a patient wait, it's these moments that make us return, again and again.

Humour in nature is never at odds with reverence; instead, it enhances it. It keeps our egos in check, our expectations soft, and our memories full of colour.

Epilogue: A Smile in the Hide

Let me end with a small scene. I was in a hide one winter morning, alone, watching a teal dabble in a frost-glazed pond. An elderly man entered, nodded, and sat beside me. We didn't speak. After a long while, he whispered, *"You know, I once tried to teach my parrot to identify waders. It only learned to say 'bloody gulls.'"*

170

We both laughed. And in that moment, nothing else was needed. The birds were there. The joy was quiet. And the world, just briefly, was thoroughly enough.

Historical Perspectives & Reflections

Throughout history, specific individuals have profoundly shaped our perception of birds and nature. Figures such as John James Audubon, Alexander von Humboldt, and Gilbert White have provided foundational insights into ornithology, natural philosophy, and wildlife. Their work continues to resonate deeply in modern bird-watching, enriching our encounters with birds and reminding us of humanity's enduring relationship with the natural world.

Famous Bird Watchers and Philosophers

Throughout history, specific individuals have profoundly shaped our perception of birds and nature. Figures such as John James Audubon, Alexander von Humboldt, Gilbert White, Rachel Carson, and Aldo Leopold have provided foundational insights into ornithology, natural philosophy, and wildlife. Their work continues to resonate deeply in modern bird-watching, enriching our encounters with birds and reminding us of humanity's enduring relationship with the natural world.

John James Audubon (1785-1851) was not only an artist but also a pioneering ornithologist whose meticulous attention to detail revolutionised how birds were illustrated and studied. Born in Haiti and raised in France, Audubon later moved to the United States, where his passion for the diverse birdlife of North America took flight. His most renowned work, *The Birds of America*, remains an extraordinary achievement, capturing the essence of American birds with unprecedented vibrancy and life-like detail.

Audubon's methods were innovative; he observed birds in their natural habitats, often for hours or days, capturing their intricate behaviours and distinctive features. His philosophical approach reflected a deep reverence for nature, viewing birds not merely as scientific specimens but as profound symbols of beauty and freedom.

Audubon's reflections in his journals offer timeless insight into the experience of bird watching. He described the solitude and peace found in quiet contemplation of birds, reminding contemporary bird watchers that patience and observation are at the heart of their pursuit.

Alexander von Humboldt (1769-1859) was a Prussian naturalist and explorer who significantly broadened humanity's understanding of nature and biodiversity. Humboldt's explorations in Latin America were groundbreaking, meticulously documenting numerous bird species alongside their ecological contexts. Unlike many contemporaries, Humboldt viewed nature holistically, recognising complex environmental interconnections. His influential work, *Cosmos*, articulated the idea that all nature is interconnected, a perspective now widely embraced but was revolutionary in his time.

Humboldt argued that studying birds and their environments could illuminate broader ecological and philosophical truths about humanity's place in nature. Today, modern bird watchers echo Humboldt's perspective, viewing birds as indicators of environmental health and thereby embodying his ecological interconnectedness.

Gilbert White (1720-1793) was an English naturalist and clergyman who made a profound contribution through his work, *The Natural History and Antiquities of Selborne*. White approached ornithology from a localised, deeply attentive perspective, meticulously documenting bird behaviours, seasonal migrations, and interactions within ecosystems. His detailed observations over decades offered insights into avian life and emphasised the importance of long-term, patient study.

White's philosophy underscored the intrinsic value of simple observation, often from his garden, revealing profound truths hidden within everyday phenomena. Bird watchers today

173

resonate with White's approach, finding significance in the mindful and sustained observation of local birdlife.

Rachel Carson (1907-1964) was an American marine biologist and conservationist, profoundly influenced environmental consciousness through her groundbreaking book, *Silent Spring*. Carson drew attention to the devastating impact of pesticides on bird populations, marking a significant shift towards ecological conservation and sustainable practices. Her work highlighted the vulnerability of birds as vital indicators of environmental balance, prompting a worldwide reconsideration of humanity's relationship with the natural world.

Aldo Leopold (1887-1948) was an American ecologist and philosopher, made significant contributions to conservation ethics through his seminal book, *A Sand County Almanack*. Leopold introduced the concept of the *"land ethic,"* advocating for a responsible, ethical relationship between people and nature, with birds often serving as symbols and practical indicators of environmental health.

Konrad Lorenz (1903–1989) was an Austrian ethologist and psychologist. Konrad Lorenz profoundly shaped our understanding of animal behaviour through his pioneering studies on imprinting and instinctive behavioural patterns, particularly in birds. Lorenz meticulously observed geese and jackdaws, uncovering the mechanisms behind imprinting. This is the process by which newly hatched birds instinctively bond with the first moving object they encounter. His classic experiment, in which goslings imprinted on Lorenz himself, vividly demonstrated this principle, opening a new field of study that connects psychology, ethology, and ornithology.

Lorenz's influential work, notably presented in *King Solomon's Ring* (1949) and *On Aggression* (1966), provided philosophical insights into the intrinsic bonds between nature and humanity, as well as the connections between humans and animals. His findings highlighted that birds not only exhibit complex emotional lives but also have behaviours deeply connected to evolutionary survival and social interaction. Lorenz believed passionately in observing animals in their natural environment to understand their behaviours and motivations genuinely. Modern bird watchers continue to benefit from Lorenz's emphasis on empathy, patience, and detailed observation, recognising the rich psychological dimensions underlying avian behaviour.

Niko Tinbergen (1907–1988) was a Dutch-British ethologist and Nobel laureate. Niko Tinbergen significantly advanced the scientific and psychological understanding of bird behaviour. Alongside Lorenz, Tinbergen is regarded as a founding figure in ethology, famous for identifying the four questions crucial to understanding animal behaviour: causation, development, evolution, and adaptive function.

Tinbergen's pioneering studies of gulls, notably the herring gull, explored instinctive behavioural responses, including nesting rituals, parental care, aggression, and territoriality. His careful observational methodologies in natural settings were revolutionary, demonstrating how complex avian behaviours evolved through adaptation. His seminal work, *The Study of Instinct* (1951), combined psychological theory, ethological observation, and philosophical reflections on human nature and animal instincts, profoundly influencing both biological psychology and conservation philosophy.

Tinbergen believed deeply that understanding animal behaviour not only enriches human appreciation of nature but also offers profound philosophical insights about human life, relationships, and psychological processes. Bird watchers today, guided by Tinbergen's methods, embrace a more profound psychological curiosity and greater scientific rigour, fostering greater empathy for avian life and environmental conservation.

Historical Perceptions of Birds: Shifts in Understanding

Human attitudes toward birds have undergone significant evolution throughout history, reflecting broader cultural shifts in understanding wildlife and the natural world. Ancient civilisations often revered birds as sacred symbols. The Egyptians saw them as divine intermediaries, while Greeks and Romans regarded them as omens or manifestations of deities.

During medieval times, perceptions shifted, often categorising birds as either pests or symbols laden with moral allegory. Birds were prominently featured in literature and art, frequently representing virtues or vices, human qualities distilled into feathered forms. This symbolic use persisted until the Enlightenment, when empirical approaches began to dominate natural sciences.

The Enlightenment brought about radical changes, as rational and empirical study displaced mythological interpretations. Birds were systematically classified and studied scientifically for the first time, laying the foundations for the field of ornithology. Works by Carl Linnaeus introduced methodical classification, greatly enhancing the scientific understanding of avian species and behaviours.

The Romantic movement of the late 18th and early 19th centuries witnessed a renewed poetic and philosophical appreciation for birds as symbols of freedom, creativity, and transcendence. This era celebrated the emotional connection to birds and nature, as captured vividly by poets such as Wordsworth, Keats, and Shelley. Their poetry reaffirmed the human emotional and spiritual relationship with birds, influencing contemporary bird watchers who seek poetic and philosophical dimensions in their practice.

How Past Philosophers Understood Nature and Wildlife

Philosophers have profoundly shaped humanity's understanding of nature and wildlife, shaping modern perceptions of birdwatching. Ancient philosophers, such as Aristotle, approached nature systematically, categorising birds scientifically and philosophically. Aristotle's *Historia Animalium* offered detailed descriptions and classifications, emphasising rational observation to understand nature's order.

Medieval philosopher St. Francis of Assisi provided a starkly contrasting perspective, emphasising spiritual unity with all creatures. His philosophy advocated humility and compassion towards animals, notably birds, which he viewed as equal participants in divine creation.

The Enlightenment philosophy of Rousseau and Voltaire heralded a new reverence for nature as morally instructive and inherently good, suggesting that reconnecting with wildlife restored humanity's innate virtues and emotional balance. Rousseau argued that birds symbolised natural freedom untouched by society's corrupting influence.

In the 19th century, transcendentalists like Thoreau and Emerson deeply impacted perceptions of nature, emphasising solitude and spiritual insight gained through quiet observation of wildlife, particularly birds. Thoreau's journals highlight the intimate relationship between human introspection and observation of birds, presenting nature as a profound teacher capable of revealing deep philosophical truths.

Nietzsche, too, metaphorically employed birds to illustrate freedom and aspiration, often using imagery of flight to represent human intellectual and existential struggles. These philosophical traditions have influenced contemporary birdwatchers, who seek a deeper understanding of themselves and the world through their interactions with birds.

Indigenous Wisdom and Bird Symbolism

Indigenous cultures have long maintained rich, meaningful traditions connecting birds to spiritual and ecological wisdom. Native American cultures, for example, attribute powerful symbolic meanings to birds. Eagles represent strength, vision, and spiritual clarity and owls are seen as keepers of sacred knowledge. These perspectives offer contemporary bird watchers deeper, symbolic connections with birds, enriching the act of observing nature with spiritual and philosophical depth.

Australian Aboriginal culture similarly connects birds closely to creation myths and landscape storytelling. Birds feature prominently in Dreamtime narratives, where species such as the Emu and the Kookaburra are celebrated as integral parts of sacred creation. Exploring these traditions provides modern bird watchers with profound insights into ecological interconnectedness and spiritual reverence.

Philosophical Insights into Nature from Antiquity to Modernity

Historical philosophers have provided profound insights into human relations with birds and nature, significantly impacting modern ecological thinking.

Aristotle offered meticulous observations of bird biology and behaviour, grounding later studies in empirical observation. His belief that careful attention to nature was foundational to knowledge influenced centuries of naturalists.

Later, philosophers like Henry David Thoreau echoed Aristotle's meticulous observations, adding a spiritual dimension, arguing that nature serves as an avenue for philosophical reflection and personal enlightenment. Thoreau's writings on nature, especially in *Walden*, highlight birds as central symbols of simplicity, freedom, and contemplation.

Similarly, Ralph Waldo Emerson believed that birds conveyed a profound spiritual message about authenticity and living in harmony with nature. His transcendentalist view suggests that birds remind humanity of our potential to transcend material concerns and reconnect with essential spiritual truths.

Reflections and Modern Connections: Learning from the Past

Reflective essays in contemporary bird-watching literature draw powerful connections between historical philosophical insights and present-day practices. The essential lessons from Audubon, Humboldt, and others emphasise the importance of patience, mindful observation, ecological interconnectedness, and ethical responsibility.

Today, climate change, biodiversity loss, and habitat destruction underscore the renewed urgency of historical lessons. Reflecting on past figures helps modern bird watchers to recognise that observing birds extends beyond individual experience to ethical awareness and ecological responsibility.

Incorporating indigenous wisdom further enriches modern perspectives, guiding bird watchers toward a deeper ecological consciousness and respect for wildlife habitats. Reflective essays encourage bird watchers not merely to observe, but to actively engage in conservation, preserving both avian biodiversity and a philosophical heritage.

The Evolution of Conservation Ethics

Bird watching today is deeply rooted in the historical conservation ethics developed by figures such as Leopold and Carson. The historical shift from exploitation and observation to active protection and stewardship marks a crucial development in ecological philosophy. Understanding this evolution inspires modern bird watchers to become actively engaged in conservation practices and citizen science initiatives, underscoring their roles as environmental stewards.

Today's bird watchers are therefore part of a historical continuum of awareness, appreciation, and action, moving beyond passive observers to become committed advocates for environmental health, biodiversity, and ethical ecological relationships.

Reflective Essays: Connecting Past Insights to Modern Bird Watching

Reflecting on historical perspectives deepens our appreciation of modern bird watching, enriching it with philosophical, ecological, and emotional dimensions. The legacies of Audubon, Humboldt, and White underscore the continuity of patient, attentive observation as a fundamental aspect of birding, while historical shifts in perception remind us of the ethical evolution underlying modern conservation principles.

A reflective contemplation inspired by Gilbert White might encourage us to appreciate the quiet revelations offered by local birds are reminders of nature's subtle and yet persistent presence. Audubon's approach might prompt us to consider birds' inherent beauty and individuality, fostering an emotional and aesthetic appreciation that extends beyond mere scientific observation.

Humboldt's holistic ecological vision resonates profoundly today, guiding bird watchers to recognise their observations within broader environmental contexts. Contemporary bird watchers, informed by these historical insights, often participate in citizen science projects, contributing to global data while embodying Humboldt's vision of interconnectedness.

Philosophical traditions similarly inspire modern bird watchers. Thoreau and Emerson's insights offer contemplative frameworks that urge bird watchers to approach their activity as a meditative practice, deepening their connection to the natural world and themselves. Nietzsche's symbolic use of birds invites introspection, allowing birdwatchers to contemplate broader existential meanings in their encounters with birds.

These reflective essays remind us that bird watching, though seemingly straightforward, engages profound philosophical and emotional depths, connecting past wisdom with present practice and grounding humanity in a deeper ecological and existential awareness.

Ultimately, historical perspectives illuminate bird watching as more than a recreational activity; it becomes a philosophical practice that encourages reflection, empathy, and ethical responsibility. By weaving these rich historical and intellectual insights into contemporary experiences, bird watchers today carry forward an enduring tradition of wonder, reverence, and ecological stewardship.

The Garden Watcher

A Ritual of Return

Each morning begins the same. I open the balcony door, step outside with a cup of tea in hand, and pause. The ritual is not dramatic; there is no pilgrimage and no distant adventure. Just the low hum of the city in the background, the scent of damp air or summer heat, and a moment of quiet from my view of the garden. It is here, in these modest grounds around our apartment, that I became not just a bird watcher, but a garden watcher, too.

This garden is a living stage. Over time, I began to learn its rhythms as intimately as my own. The clumsy arrival of a blackbird, tail fanned and wings shuddering as it lands with the sudden thrill of blue tits navigating the buddleia. A robin appeared as if summoned, standing proud on the birdhouse with its head tilted in familiar curiosity. These moments have become daily companions.

Unlike the thrill of spotting a rare migrant on windswept cliffs, the garden watch is a slow process. It is unhurried, repetitive, and intimate. And in that slowness, it becomes something else; it is a ritual of return. Not just a return to place, but to self.

Notes from the Seasons

Spring is the most dramatic transformation. One morning in March, the stillness cracks open as song thrushes return to their aria, wood-pigeons become amorous, and the entire garden lifts its head. With the shifting light comes the promise of change. Nest-building begins with frantic haste. I once watched a great tit carry a feather, twice its size, back and forth for over an hour, indecisive about its placement. A quiet perfectionism, perhaps.

In summer, the garden hums with activity. The borders fill with butterflies, bees, and the soft ticking of wings. Blackcaps sing from the elder tree, and the fledglings arrive in fluttering waves, who are unsure of flight, and are certain of hunger. I've spent many mornings watching a pair of goldfinches feed their young, each arrival met with squeaking insistence. There's a beauty in their clumsiness.

Autumn is quieter, but no less profound. As the flowers fade, movement slows. Jays begin hiding acorns in the borders. The robins reassert territorial dominance with an elegance that almost masks the violence. By October, the garden has already started to thin out slightly, leaving space for reflection and memory.

And then winter. It is a time of minimalism. A single wren appears in the frost. A blackbird's song takes on an eerie clarity in the cold. The garden stripped back to the essentials, asking nothing, yet offering everything.

The Extraordinary in the Ordinary

The philosopher Gaston Bachelard once wrote that the house is our first universe. If that is so, then the garden is its border with the cosmos. It is the threshold where the human and the wild coexist. Bird watching in the garden is, in this way, not a hobby but a quiet philosophical act.

There is a danger in overlooking the ordinary in a world obsessed with novelty, where the garden dares to be repetitive. But repetition, like a mantra, becomes meaningful over time. The daily appearance of the same robin is grounding. The small drama of a coal tit outwitting a woodpecker at the feeder becomes a lesson in ingenuity. The sound of sparrows arguing in the hedge is a song of domestic familiarity.

To watch garden birds is to practice a kind of radical attention. It is to look without seeking spectacle. It is to say: *"This moment, this bird, this rustling of leaves; this is enough."* It reminds us that the extraordinary is not elsewhere. It is right here, in the rustle of wings and the stillness of being.

Psychological Anchoring

There is something undeniably soothing in watching birds. Studies in environmental psychology have shown that regular exposure to nature, especially nearby nature, can reduce stress, lower blood pressure, and even improve concentration and emotional regulation. But the garden watcher does not need studies to know this. We feel it.

The predictability of daily bird visits acts as a counterweight to the chaos of the world. The constancy of the great tit, the sudden cheer of a wren, the elegance of a dunnock's shuffle along the base of the hedge as each act stabilises us. In times of uncertainty, the garden becomes a sanctuary of known rhythms.

For those with limited mobility or those dealing with grief, anxiety, or isolation, the garden can be a profound source of comfort. The presence of birds offers a connection without demand. You do not need to impress a blackbird. You need to be present.

During difficult periods of my life, I found it easier to face the day if I had seen the robin. His presence, punctual and expectant, gave the morning a shape. I have heard similar stories from others, where elderly neighbours talk to their blue tits, children name the pigeons, and carers say the garden gives their patients a reason to rise and go outside.

It is, in its simplest form, the therapy of observation.

Stories from the Garden

In our and other surrounding gardens, I have accumulated years 'worth of stories. There was the year the sparrows nested in the ivy and launched a miniature air force each morning from the wall. There was the curious friendship between a magpie and our neighbour's cat, such that they would sit side by side for long periods without moving. There was the time a goldcrest, barely the size of a thumb, appeared in the apple tree during a cold snap, blinking like a visitor from another realm.

One spring, I watched a blackbird learn to take raisins from the back step of a house opposite. It began with hesitancy. Then confidence. Then, a kind of entitlement. By summer, he was knocking on the window if I was late.

These stories are not grand. But they are layered with meaning. They become part of the family lore. And over time, they add up to a form of belonging, not just in place, but also in time.

Garden as Public Space

Not all gardens are private. Across cities and towns, community gardens have become spaces of shared care and community engagement. And in these places, birds often serve as the first bridge between strangers. A goldfinch landing on a shared sunflower can begin a conversation between two people who have never spoken. A nest found in a shed becomes a communal secret. The feeders must be filled. The compost must be protected from the squirrels.

Birds become mediators in a shared ecology of attention.

In the next neighbourhood, a small communal garden project, initially designed to support pollinators, quickly became a haven for house sparrows, blackbirds, and robins. Now, it also hosts art classes, tea mornings, and bird-friendly planting workshops. What began as environmental stewardship has grown into emotional infrastructure.

Watching birds together removes hierarchy. It doesn't matter who you are; if you can be still, if you can notice, you belong.

Backyard Conservation

Small actions matter, like putting out water during heatwaves, planting native shrubs, and leaving a corner of the garden wild, which are acts of micro-conservation.

Garden watchers are often the first to notice changes in the garden. Fewer starlings this year. An early arrival of the chiffchaff. The worrying silence after Silvester (New Year) fireworks. These observations, when shared, become valuable data. In the UK, the RSPB's Big Garden Birdwatch has become one of the most significant citizen science projects in the world. And it relies not on professionals in remote locations, but on people like us, sitting with tea in the garden.

The garden becomes not just a site of watching, but of care. And through that care, a form of resistance. In an age of climate crisis, watching birds in the garden is not only an escape but also a powerful statement. It is a commitment to noticing, to protecting, and to belonging.

The Garden as a Mirror

One humbling experience is becoming a garden watcher. Over time, the birds begin to reflect our moods, seasons, and needs.

When I am anxious, I notice how easily the birds scatter. Yet, when I am calm, they return. When I am impatient, I miss them entirely. But when I sit with stillness, they come closer than I imagined possible.

They do not demand that I solve the world's problems. They ask only that I notice. That I take seriously the quiet miracle of their presence.

In this way, bird watching in the garden becomes a mirror. A form of self-awareness. And a path toward presence.

A Quiet Revolution

The garden watcher is not flashy. We do not boast long species lists or travel far for rare sightings. But we have something else: a depth of attention. We know our robins by their breast markings, our blackbirds by their song.

And in a world moving ever faster, that kind of attention is quietly revolutionary.

To watch the same garden day after day, season after season, is to enter into a relationship. It means: I see you. I will be here tomorrow. I will keep watching.

And in that watching, we find a form of belonging that no map can offer a home in place, in time, in memory, and care.

Micro-Migrations and Familiar Strangers

In mid-September, I often notice a subtle shift. There's a pause in the usual routine, as if the garden, for a moment, holds its breath. Then, just before dusk, a soft chattering comes from the treetop. A party of long-tailed tits has arrived.

They are not regulars in the garden, but familiar strangers who are migrants of the local landscape, drifting from one patch of green to another like laughter caught in the wind. When they pass through, they come in numbers, perhaps ten, twelve, or sometimes more. The tiny bodies with pinstripe tails, pinging calls, and a restlessness that leaves the buddleia quivering. They never stay long. Maybe for fifteen minutes of chaotic grace, and they're gone.

I've grown to anticipate their visits, which mark the season's turn, better than any calendar. And even though they come uninvited, there's always a quiet joy in their return. They remind me that the garden is not mine. Instead, it is a stopover, a node in a network far beyond my understanding. And that, somehow, makes it even more sacred.

The Philosophy of Scale

We are conditioned to seek meaning in vast landscapes, dramatic events, and sweeping changes. However, the garden invites us into another realm of the miniature, the overlooked, and the close at hand.

This is where we learn what the philosopher Simone Weil might call *attentive love.* To love the world not as we wish it to be, but as it is in its smallness and its imperfection, all within its rhythms.

Maybe it is in the soft scratching of a dunnock beneath the cotoneaster, or in the fat bee thudding against the bird bath. In the way a feathered wing curls against the chest as a pigeon preens in the sun.

I once watched a goldfinch stand still for nearly five minutes. There was no song and no movement. There was just stillness, a breathing sculpture among the teasel. At first, I thought something was wrong. But then I realised it was simply being. And in that moment, so was I.

The garden reminds us that life happens in the margins. That attention is not a means to an end. It is the end itself.

Intimacy with the Local

In northern Germany, our garden flora is shaped by a temperate maritime climate. Winters are cold but not brutal. Summers are mild, though warming with the years. The plantings here, which are a mix of hazel, holly, rosehips, cornflower, elder, and wild thyme, support a diverse local ecology.

Our garden borders a hedge of hawthorn and privet. In spring, the hawthorn blossoms fill the air with scent and hum with life with hoverflies, bumblebees and green bottle flies. This hedge is a bird metropolis. Sparrows' nest deep inside, their young cheeping for weeks. Blue tits bounce through the foliage like animated punctuation marks.

A pair of black redstarts nested in a gap in the brickwork one year. At first, I mistook them for robins, but their sooty plumage and fluttering perches gave them away. Their calls, a soft, like gravel on silk, woke me each morning that summer. They stayed there until the leaves fell.

There's also the fox. He doesn't live in the garden, but he passes through with careful dignity. At dusk, when the light is low and the sky blushes, he slips between the hedge roots. The birds fall silent, but they do not panic. He trots across the lawn like a ghost. We've watched each other many times, he and I. Each is wondering what the other is doing here.

This daily familiarity with the local, or what anthropologists might call *"dwelling-in-place"*, creates a form of knowing that is different from academic knowledge. It is about a relationship between the two.

On Naming and Knowing

We often name the birds we see regularly. The robin becomes *"Red,"* the blackbird *"Bruno,"* the pair of collared doves *"the Lovers."* It is a childish act, in the best sense, as it infuses the world with personality and presence.

Naming creates intimacy. But it also raises questions. What do we know when we give a personal name to something? And what do we overlook? The philosopher Martin Buber distinguished between two ways of relating: *"I-It"* and *"I-Thou."* In the garden, we often begin with *"I-It"* observation, focusing on birds as objects of study or entertainment. But over time, something shifts. We enter into *"I-Thou"* relationships, in which the bird is no longer a thing, but a being.

You begin to notice a pattern of how one robin is bolder than another, how one tit prefers the peanut feeder while another likes the suet balls. These are not scientific observations; they are relational.

189

In this way, the garden becomes a training ground in the ethics of attention. It teaches us how to see ourselves as co-inhabitants of the world.

The Psychology of Home

Bird-watching in the garden has become an integral part of my daily routine, shaping my day and settling my mind. It offers a sense of home, psychologically.

Clinical psychologist Dr Paul Gilbert has spoken of *"soothing systems"* in the brain, the neurological states that counteract threat and drive. Watching birds activates these systems. It slows the heart. It brings the mind into the present. Fortunately, it does not require high performance.

In times of personal upheaval, I've found myself returning to the garden with a kind of instinct. When my mother was ill, I would spend long stretches simply sitting by the bird bath, watching the starlings wash and preen, aggressive and joyful. I didn't realise it then, but I was healing.

In his book *The Nature Fix*, Florence Williams shows how even brief exposure to nature can regulate mood, improve memory, and build emotional resilience. The garden is our most accessible dose of this medicine.

A Living Diary

I once kept a notebook near the balcony door. Each morning, I'd jot down what I saw: *"Robin appeared at 07:10. Jay was in the birch. Crows are debating in the tree."* At first, it was an act of documentation. However, over time, it evolved into a kind of diary for the birds and for myself.

The entries began to reflect more than sightings. *"Felt anxious this morning, but calmed after watching the dunnock for ten minutes through the grey sky. There was no movement, but then the woodpecker appeared, like a blessing."*

The act of writing became a bridge between inner and outer landscapes. And now, much later, the notebook serves as a kind of mirror. I can look back and see not only what birds were present, but who I was becoming.

Generations of Watchers

My uncle was a keen birdwatcher in the garden. He lived in Yorkshire, in a modest house with a back garden. Every morning, he would shuffle out with a biscuit tin full of seed and scatter it in careful arcs. He had names for the birds. *"That's Mopsy,"* he once said, pointing to a goldfinch with a bent leg. *"She's been coming here for several weeks, now."*

I sometimes wonder how many people have stood where I now stand with tea in hand, eyes scanning the branches, and heart quieted by the flicker of wings. The act connects us across time. It is one of the few rituals that has remained unchanged amid endless change.

The Garden as Sanctuary and Resistance

To care for a garden is to resist the cultural narrative of urgency. It is to slow down and to say: this place matters.

Bird-watching in the garden becomes a sanctuary for the birds and for ourselves. In a world where screens dominate and attention is monetised, simply sitting and noticing is a radical act. Ecopsychologist Mary-Jayne Rust writes about *"ecological selfhood,"* which is the idea that our identity is not separate from nature but is interwoven with it. In the garden, this becomes a lived truth. I am not just watching birds. I am participating in a shared world.

And this participation can extend outward. A neighbour once saw my wife watching the goldfinches and asked what they were. The following week, she bought a feeder. Now, she watches too.

191

Sometimes we compare notes when we see each other. Slowly, the garden becomes networked with a patchwork of care.

A Closing Reflection

There is a moment, just after dusk, when the garden falls silent. The birds have gone to roost as the air cools and the leaves fall still.

It is then that I feel the deepest form of gratitude for its presence. For the chance to belong to a place through attention to what I have seen and heard.

I once read that *"to love something is to learn its rhythms."* The garden has taught me this truth. It has trained my eyes to see the beauty of a rusted feeder, the choreography of sparrows, along with the quiet dignity of the hedge.

And in doing so, it has shown me something else: the world is not elsewhere. It is here. Beneath the hawthorn. Beside the compost. In the flick of a wing and the sound of a robin's song.

It's all around us.

To watch the garden is to remember what it means to live.

The Watch Continues

There is no final sighting: no definitive bird and no moment of perfect stillness that closes the book on a life of watching. Instead, there is the slow unfolding of presence. And then, if you're lucky, the sense that it unfolds again tomorrow.

This book began with a borrowed pair of binoculars and a marsh harrier drifting across the hush of Minsmere. But it was never just about that bird, or that place. It was about attention. It was about what happens to a life when it slows down enough to listen, to the flap of the wings, to the changes of the weather, to the wonder of nature.

Across these pages, we have explored flight and patience, ethics and joy, humour and grief. We have met strangers in hides and familiar birds on fences. We have looked up, again and again, and found something waiting there that is not always visible, not always nameable, but always alive.

So, how do we end?

Perhaps we don't.

Because bird watching, at its heart, resists endings. It does not offer resolution. Instead, it provides a return. Rather than a grand conclusion, it offers a daily invitation: *Look again.* Listen. Be still. The bird might come, or it might not. But either way, you will have watched.

And in watching, something in you will have stayed open.

A Practice, Not a Performance

The more profound truth of bird watching hums beneath the pages of every chapter: it is not a skill to master, but a practice to inhabit. There is no final test. No moment when one becomes *"a real birder."* Only a widening capacity to notice, to care, to wait.

There is something beautiful in that. Something resistant to modern life's obsession with productivity and closure. Bird watching teaches us that not every hour must produce something. That beauty is not earned. That value can live in the unseen.

And in this way, bird watching becomes a philosophy. A way of resisting what dehumanises us. A way of remembering what restores us. Not of escape, but of return.

The Sky Is Still Open

The birds will keep flying across oceans and alleyways, over war zones and wildflowers, and through cities and memory.

Some will vanish. Some will recover. Some will change their routes entirely, following new wind patterns and altered seasons. But always, there will be something to witness. Something to hold in view, and then to release.

And we, the watchers, will change too.

We will grow older. Our knees might ache. Our vision might blur. But if we can still lift our heads, still pause at a window, carry a moment of stillness in our chest, then we can still watch.

Even without names.
Even without sound.
Even without answers.

One Last Image

Let me leave you with this: a small bird, no bigger than a hand, perched on the tip of a bent reed at dusk. The sky is grey-gold. The wind is barely moving. You are alone, or perhaps not. It doesn't matter.

You watch.
You breathe.

And for a moment, the bird turns its head, not toward the sun, not toward the trees, but toward you.

There is no message in this. And there is no metaphor to unpack. Only the fact of shared presence. The brief miracle of being alive at the same time, in the same place, under the same sky.

Then the bird lifts off. And you remain.

Still watching.

Epilogue: Keep Looking

Wherever you are, whether you are on a balcony, in a forest, beside a canal, on a cliff edge or at a bus stop, keep looking. Let your gaze be soft and let your breath be slow.

Remember: you don't need to find the rarest bird to be moved. You don't need to know the name. You only need to care enough to stop. The world is still unfolding.

The sky is still open.
The watch continues.
So go.
And see what you will see.

Master Reference List

The Mindful Watcher

Primary References
Epictetus – *Discourses*, Stoic reflections on acceptance.
Marcus Aurelius – *Meditations*, on patience, presence, and nature.
Zen Buddhist texts – especially on *shikantaza* ("just sitting") and *kenshō* (glimpses of true nature).
BioScience study – linking bird-rich areas with mental well-being.
Psychological studies – on birdsong reducing anxiety and depression.

Secondary References
Jon Kabat-Zinn – *Wherever You Go, There You Are*, mindfulness in everyday life.
Thích Nhat Hanh – *The Miracle of Mindfulness*, teachings on presence.
Florence Williams – *The Nature Fix*, on nature's healing effects.

A Skyward Gaze (Flight as Freedom)

Primary References
Edgar Allan Poe – *The Raven*, a haunting meditation on grief.
Friedrich Nietzsche – *Thus Spoke Zarathustra*, with its eagle and serpent imagery.
Jean-Paul Sartre – *Being and Nothingness*, on radical freedom and responsibility.
Albert Camus – *The Myth of Sisyphus*, freedom through defiance of the absurd.

Secondary References
Robert Solomon – *Existentialism*, an overview of existentialist thought.
Julian Young – *Nietzsche's Philosophy of Religion*, on Nietzsche's symbols and imagery.
Thomas Flynn – *Sartre and Existentialism*, context and interpretation.

The Aesthetics of Bird Watching

Primary References
Immanuel Kant – *Critique of Judgment*, on beauty and the sublime.
Arthur Schopenhauer – *The World as Will and Representation*, on aesthetic perception.
Edmund Burke – *On the Sublime and Beautiful*, early reflections on awe.
Maurice Merleau-Ponty – *Phenomenology of Perception*, seeing as embodied participation.

Secondary References
Allen Carlson – *Nature and Landscape: An Introduction to Environmental Aesthetics*.
Emily Brady – *The Sublime in Modern Philosophy*.
Dacher Keltner – research on awe and the "small self."

The Ethics of Bird Watching

Primary References
Aldo Leopold – *A Sand County Almanack*, the "land ethic."
Arne Næss – *Ecology, Community and Lifestyle*, the founding text of Deep Ecology.
American Birding Association – *Code of Birding Ethics*.
Cornell Lab of Ornithology – *eBird*, citizen science in action.

Secondary References
Peter Singer – *Practical Ethics*.
Holmes Rolston – *Environmental Ethics*.
Rachel Carson – *Silent Spring*, a prophetic call for ecological care.

A Life Shaped by Watching

Primary References
Gaston Bachelard – *The Poetics of Space*, on intimacy and belonging.
Psychological literature – on identity, belonging, and the shaping of the self.

Secondary References
Richard Louv – *Last Child in the Woods*, on nature and identity.
Diane Ackerman – *The Moon by Whale Light*, essays on nature's wonder.
Michael McCarthy – *The Moth Snowstorm*, on joy and environmental loss.

Time, Patience, and Observation

Primary References
Heraclitus – fragments on change and time.
Henri Bergson – *Time and Free Will*, distinguishing clock time from lived duration.
Martin Heidegger – *Being and Time*, time as the structure of being.
Simone Weil – *Waiting for God*, attention as devotion.
Viktor Frankl – *Man's Search for Meaning*, the space between stimulus and response.
Stephen & Rachel Kaplan – *The Experience of Nature*, attention restoration theory.
Mihaly Csikszentmihalyi – *Flow*, on absorption and presence.

Secondary References

Barbara Adam – *Timewatch: The Social Analysis of Time*.
Oliver Sacks – *The River of Consciousness*, reflections on time and mind.

Technology in Bird Watching

Primary References

Roger Tory Peterson – *A Field Guide to the Birds*, a revolution in identification.
Albert Borgmann – *Technology and the Character of Contemporary Life*.
Martin Heidegger – "The Question Concerning Technology."
Bruno Latour – *We Have Never Been Modern*.
Rachel Carson – *The Sense of Wonder*, on science and awe.

Secondary References

Sherry Turkle – *Alone Together*, technology and presence.
Berenice Miller – *Birding and Technology*.
BirdNET, Merlin, Xeno-Canto, eBird – platforms shaping modern birding.

Cultural Perspectives and Symbolism

Primary References

Ernst Cassirer – *An Essay on Man*, symbolism as a framework of meaning.
Carl Jung – *Man and His Symbols*, archetypes and the collective unconscious.
Myths and traditions – Icarus, Odin's ravens, Quetzalcoatl, Garuda, Aboriginal Dreamtime, among others.

Secondary References

Karen Armstrong – *A Short History of Myth*.
Mircea Eliade – *Myth and Reality*.
Joseph Campbell – *The Hero with a Thousand Faces*.

Bird Watching Holidays & International Adventures

Primary References
Martin Buber – *I and Thou*, encounters as a relationship.
Simone Weil – writings on attention.
Henry David Thoreau – *Walden*; *Walking*, on presence in nature.

Secondary References
Robert Macfarlane – *The Wild Places*.
Frédéric Gros – *A Philosophy of Walking*.
Alain de Botton – *The Art of Travel*.

Citizen Science & Environmental Awareness

Primary References
Frank M. Chapman – originator of the Audubon Christmas Bird Count (1900).
Cornell Lab of Ornithology – *eBird*.
Arne Næss – *Deep Ecology*.
Rachel Carson – *Silent Spring*.

Secondary References
Rick Bonney et al. – *Citizen Science: Public Participation in Environmental Research*.
Abraham Miller-Rushing et al. – "The Role of Citizen Science in Ecology and Conservation," *Ecological Applications*.
Piet Strydom – *Green Thought in Sociology*.

Inclusivity & Accessibility in Bird Watching

Primary References
Martha C. Nussbaum – *Frontiers of Justice*, on justice and capabilities.

Iris Marion Young – *Justice and the Politics of Difference*, grounding for inclusivity.
bell hooks – *Belonging: A Culture of Place*, on community and nature.
Tom Shakespeare – *Disability Rights and Wrongs*, accessibility as social practice.
Environmental psychology research – on belonging, inclusion, and safety.

Secondary References
J. Drew Lanham – *The Home Place: Memoirs of a Colored Man's Love Affair with Nature*.
Christian Cooper – *Better Living Through Birding: Notes from a Black Man in the Natural World*.
Richard Louv – *Last Child in the Woods*, on accessibility of nature for children.
Birdability movement – resources on inclusive birding practices.
Audubon Society articles – on diversity and accessibility in birding communities.

Humour, Joy, and Quirky Encounters

Primary References
Ralph Waldo Emerson – *Works and Essays*, source of "The earth laughs in flowers."
Georges Bataille – writings on laughter as rupture and communion with the sacred.
Henri Bergson – *Laughter: An Essay on the Meaning of the Comic*.
Thích Nhất Hanh – *Peace is Every Step*, teachings on joy as presence.
Positive psychology research – on humour, gratitude, and resilience.

Secondary References
Simon Barnes – *How to Be a Bad Birdwatcher*, a playful take on joy.

Mark Cocker – *Birders: Tales of a Tribe*, humorous portraits of birding culture.
Sy Montgomery – *Birdology*, quirky encounters with birds.
John Wright – *The Naming of the Shrew*, on eccentricities of naming nature.
Anecdotal birding literature – stories of humour in natural history writing.

Historical Perspectives & Reflections

Primary References
Gilbert White – *The Natural History of Selborne*, early naturalist reflections.
John James Audubon – *Birds of America*, art and observation.
Alexander von Humboldt – *Cosmos*, holistic ecological vision.
Henry David Thoreau – *Walden*; *Walking*, meditations on nature.
Ralph Waldo Emerson – *Nature*, transcendentalist insights into wildness.

Secondary References
Andrea Wulf – *The Invention of Nature*, on Humboldt's worldview.
Robert Macfarlane – *Landmarks*, reflections on language and place.
Jenny Uglow – *Nature's Engraver: A Life of Thomas Bewick*.
Stephen Moss – *A History of Birdwatching in 100 Objects*.
Jonathan Bate – *Romantic Ecology*, on poetry, nature, and philosophy.

The Garden Watcher

Primary References
Gaston Bachelard – *The Poetics of Space*, on intimacy and home.

Rainer Maria Rilke – *Selected Poems*, reflections on everyday presence.

Mary Oliver – *Devotions* and other poems, on daily nature and attention.

Maurice Merleau-Ponty – *Phenomenology of Perception*, on embodied seeing.

Gilbert White – garden observations.

Henry David Thoreau – *Walden*; *Walking*.

Secondary References

Roger Deakin – *Notes from Walnut Tree Farm*, reflections on local living.

Richard Mabey – *Nature Cure*, personal healing and near-at-hand wild.

Anna Pavord – *The Tulip* and essays on seasonal cycles.

Mark Cocker – *Claxton: Field Notes from a Small Planet*.

Contemporary urban nature writing – on gardens and city-wild encounters.

Gary Snyder – *The Practice of the Wild*.

David Abram – *The Spell of the Sensuous*.

Glossary of Birding & Citizen Science Apps

eBird

Developed by the Cornell Lab of Ornithology, eBird is the world's largest bird observation platform. Birders can log sightings, upload photos and audio, and contribute to a global database that supports scientific research and conservation. It also provides real-time maps of migration and species distribution.

BirdNET

Created through a collaboration between Cornell Lab and Chemnitz University of Technology, BirdNET uses artificial intelligence to identify birds by their songs and calls. Users record audio on their phone, and the app suggests possible matches. It's especially helpful for beginners or in regions where visual sightings are difficult.

Merlin Bird ID

Another Cornell Lab project, Merlin, is designed as a user-friendly digital field guide. It helps identify birds through photos, sound recordings, and simple guided questions about size, colour, and behaviour. The app includes regional *"bird packs"* for offline use, making it practical for field use.

Xeno-Canto

An open-access, crowdsourced repository of bird sounds from around the globe. Birders and scientists upload recordings, creating a vast audio library. The app/website allows users to search by species, region, or call type, and is widely used for research, learning, and identification practice.

iNaturalist

A community-powered app for identifying and logging all kinds of biodiversity, not just birds. Users upload photos or recordings, and the community, alongside AI tools, helps confirm identifications. Observations feed into scientific datasets (e.g., GBIF), making it both a learning tool and a conservation resource.

www.ingramcontent.com/pod-product-compliance
Lightning Source LLC
Chambersburg PA
CBHW051721020426
42333CB00014B/1092